New Directions for
Teaching and Learning

Marilla D. Svinicki
EDITOR-IN-CHIEF

R. Eugene Rice
CONSULTING EDITOR

P9-DEF-853

Advancing Faculty Learning Through Interdisciplinary Collaboration

Elizabeth G. Creamer
Lisa R. Lattuca

EDITORS

Number 102 • Summer 2005
Jossey-Bass
San Francisco

ADVANCING FACULTY LEARNING THROUGH INTERDISCIPLINARY COLLABORATION
Elizabeth G. Creamer, Lisa R. Lattuca (eds.)
New Directions for Teaching and Learning, no. 102
Marilla D. Svinicki, Editor-in-Chief
R. Eugene Rice, Consulting Editor

Microfilm copies of issues and articles are available in 16mm and 35mm, as well as microfiche in 105mm, through University Microfilms Inc., 300 North Zeeb Road, Ann Arbor, Michigan 48106-1346.

NEW DIRECTIONS FOR TEACHING AND LEARNING (ISSN 0271-0633, electronic ISSN 1536-0768) is part of The Jossey-Bass Higher and Adult Education Series and is published quarterly by Wiley Subscription Services, Inc., A Wiley Company, at Jossey-Bass, 989 Market Street, San Francisco, California 94103-1741. Periodicals postage paid at San Francisco, California, and at additional mailing offices. POSTMASTER: Send address changes to New Directions for Teaching and Learning, Jossey-Bass, 989 Market Street, San Francisco, California 94103-1741.

New Directions for Teaching and Learning is indexed in College Student Personnel Abstracts, Contents Pages in Education, and Current Index to Journals in Education (ERIC).

SUBSCRIPTIONS cost $80 for individuals and $170 for institutions, agencies, and libraries. Prices subject to change. See order form at end of book.

EDITORIAL CORRESPONDENCE should be sent to the editor-in-chief, Marilla D. Svinicki, Department of Educational Psychology, University of Texas at Austin, One University Station, D5800, Austin, TX 78712.

www.josseybass.com

CONTENTS

FROM THE SERIES EDITOR

About This Publication. Since 1980, *New Directions for Teaching and Learning (NDTL)* has brought a unique blend of theory, research, and practice to leaders in postsecondary education. *NDTL* sourcebooks strive not only for solid substance but also for timeliness, compactness, and accessibility.

The series has four goals: to inform readers about current and future directions in teaching and learning in postsecondary education, to illuminate the context that shapes these new directions, to illustrate these new directions through examples from real settings, and to propose ways in which these new directions can be incorporated into still other settings.

This publication reflects the view that teaching deserves respect as a high form of scholarship. We believe that significant scholarship is conducted not only by researchers who report results of empirical investigations but also by practitioners who share disciplined reflections about teaching. Contributors to *NDTL* approach questions of teaching and learning as seriously as they approach substantive questions in their own disciplines, and they deal not only with pedagogical issues but also with the intellectual and social context in which these issues arise. Authors deal on the one hand with theory and research and on the other with practice, and they translate from research and theory to practice and back again.

About This Volume. This volume addresses a new movement in higher education to return to the original concept of a university as a place where cross-disciplinary work is the norm. More institutions are encouraging faculty to reach across disciplinary boundaries for cutting-edge research and teaching. This volume discusses what that might mean for faculty and students alike.

Marilla D. Svinicki
Editor-in-Chief

MARILLA D. SVINICKI is associate professor of educational psychology at the University of Texas at Austin.

Editors' Notes

The project that is now this volume crystallized when Elizabeth Creamer, Lisa Lattuca, Marilyn Amey, and Anna Neumann met to prepare for a symposium we were soon to present at the Association for the Study of Higher Education 2002 National Conference in Sacramento, California. Our own excitement that November day in 2002 and the enthusiasm of the audience for the ideas that emerged during the symposium propelled us to expand our thinking and writing and to invite others to join us in the production of this volume. We think that reframing interdisciplinary collaboration as about learning and the co-construction of knowledge rather than about efficiencies in practice is the unique contribution of this volume.

This volume uses a family of learning theories as a lens to explore various dimensions of faculty work. After introducing the argument in Chapter One and establishing the theoretical basis for thinking about faculty learning in Chapter Two, we explore faculty learning as it is embodied in three case studies, each focusing on a different aspect of faculty work: service or outreach in Chapter Three, research in Chapter Four, and teaching in Chapter Five. The final two chapters offer a meta-analysis of the cases to demonstrate contexts for when and how learning occurs. Chapter Six discusses the implications of the preceding chapters and introduces discussion about how to evaluate collaboratively produced work.

The audiences for this volume are academic leaders committed to faculty development and to creating hiring, promotion, and tenure policies that reward a wide range of scholarly activities. It should also be instructive to graduate students and faculty seeking to initiate or sustain interdisciplinary collaborations.

One way to judge the effectiveness of a collaborative effort is by the synergy it creates and the projects it spawns. In Elizabeth's case, the dialogue that emerged around this project led a paradigm shift from an effort to identify models of collaborative practice to the conviction that while there is a strong link between the process collaborators use and what they produce, no one model can be extracted from any context and used to distinguish effective from less effective collaborations. Lisa has used learning theory to explain how faculty members pursue curriculum reform efforts in undergraduate education. Marilyn Amey and Dennis Brown completed a book project that expands on the model they present in Chapter Three. Anna Neumann continues her research with faculty at midcareer and her exploration of factors that promote faculty growth and development. We invited Michele Minnis and Vera John-Steiner to join us later in the project, but Vera's work, including a coauthored publication with Michele, was instrumental in our early discussions about the contribution of sociocultural theory to understanding the link between collaboration, creativity, and new insight.

One of the recommendations made in the final chapter is that coauthors be transparent with readers about the roles they played in preparing a publication. Elizabeth initiated both the proposal for the symposium and for the volume, but that would not have been possible without Lisa's expertise in learning theories and interdisciplinarity. Both took the lead in two of the chapters, and each edited all of the chapters. Responsibility for the final steps of pulling the volume together was largely Elizabeth's.

The initial presentation and process of creating this volume created the kind of synergy that often energizes faculty work. The collaborative process we used to produce this volume and the kind described within it are one in the same. The ideas presented here emerged from mutual education and the integration of our individual perspectives.

Elizabeth G. Creamer
Lisa R. Lattuca
Editors

ELIZABETH G. CREAMER *is associate professor of educational research and evaluation in the Department of Educational Research and Policy Studies at Virginia Tech in Blacksburg, Virginia.*

LISA R. LATTUCA *is assistant professor and research associate in the Center for the Study of Higher Education at Pennsylvania State University in University Park, Pennsylvania.*

*This chapter defines key terms and orients readers to the
ideas explored in the rest of this volume.*

Learning as Professional Practice

Lisa R. Lattuca, Elizabeth G. Creamer

Collaboration is typically thought of in instrumental terms. College and university faculty collaborate when they need to get things done. They partner with other faculty when research projects are too complex for an individual working alone to conceptualize and conduct. They agree to team-teach when courses require contributions from experts with different knowledge bases and perspectives. They work with others when service or outreach projects focus on the multidimensional needs of a particular community and demand collaboration rather than individual consultation.

In this instrumental view, collaboration allows faculty to accomplish a set of tasks efficiently and effectively. It is a means to an end, and the processes by which individuals collaborate are largely invisible to those outside the collaboration. For the most part, processes are important to the extent that they hasten or impede the production of the expected deliverables. A focus on the products of faculty work is understandable from a number of perspectives, for example, from those of individual collaborators concerned with writing for publication, promotion, and tenure, as well as from the standpoint of administrators concerned with productivity, accountability, and rewards. However, an instrumental view of collaboration has its limits. In concentrating on deliverables, we overlook the learning that occurs as faculty produce what is delivered.

In this volume, we address the limitations of an instrumental focus on collaboration and examine the reasons that higher education stakeholders should refocus attention on faculty learning. Before proceeding with the task of exploring interdisciplinary collaborations as learning experiences, we lay some necessary groundwork.

Definitions

We begin with definitions of three key terms: *learning, interdisciplinarity,* and *collaboration.*

Learning. We define *learning* as the personal and shared construction of knowledge. Learners are active participants in their worlds who seek to create personal meanings of their experiences. In keeping with the sociocultural perspective, we also acknowledge that individuals are active participants in social environments that have accepted meanings and values that are not only learned but affect learning and what is learned. Consequently, much of what we learn, we learn from our interactions with others.

This view of learning leads us to emphasize its situated nature. To study learning, we must explore and understand how it is situated within sets of interconnected contexts. For faculty, work-related learning is often situated within disciplines and fields that comprise professional communities of national or international scope; within institutional arrangements such as departments, undergraduate and graduate degree programs, and research centers; and within a variety of social groupings such as program faculties, teaching teams, and research collaborations. We also must recognize that faculty learning is influenced by larger social contexts; our forms of inquiry and the kinds of questions we ask of the world are shaped by prevailing cultural conditions, practices, and beliefs.

Our definition of learning is appropriate for an examination of interdisciplinary collaborations because these types of collaborative activities typically require faculty to apprehend, understand, and use concepts, theories, and methods from disciplines or fields other than their own. Such interactions with other fields are always social because they require faculty members to engage with either human representatives of different academic cultures and communities of practice or with the cultural tools (disciplinary languages, methodologies, conventions) created and used by those working in these disciplines or fields.

Faculty members engaged in interdisciplinary collaboration must create new ways of working together, as well as develop new ways to perceive and understand the phenomenon of interest to them. The creative nature of interdisciplinary collaboration is therefore multifaceted. It is substantive *and* procedural, and in terms of sociocultural theory, the interplay between substance and procedure is critical to what is learned and how it is learned.

Interdisciplinarity. We have adapted the definition in which *interdisciplinary* is an adjective describing interactions among two or more different disciplines (Organisation for Economic Cooperation and Development, 1972). We broaden this definition so that it includes academic fields that are themselves multidisciplinary or interdisciplinary, such as education, social work, astrophysics, women's studies, and environmental science. To these, we add perspectives, such as postmodernism and critical theory, that may or may not be discipline based but clearly influence the way faculty understand and approach their teaching, research, and service obligations.

Different types of interactions are at the heart of this definition. Interactions can "range from simple communication of ideas to the mutual integration of organizing concepts, methodology, procedures, epistemology, terminology, data, and organization of research and education in a fairly large field" (Organisation for Economic Cooperation and Development, 1972, p. 25). This breadth enables us to include joint learning activities that at the onset have a limited scope but evolve to become both interdisciplinary and collaborative.

Collaboration. Like the word *interdisciplinary,* the word *collaboration* is used to refer to a broad range of activities. Most definitions focus on procedural issues and assume that the primary advantage or outcome of collaboration is that it allows efficiencies gained by a clear division of labor. But we jettison an instrumental focus and a prescription about what is required to achieve it, believing the collaborative patterns are probably as idiosyncratic as the endless combinations of people who pursue them. We define collaboration *as a social inquiry practice that promotes learning.* By using the word *social,* we are placing interaction and relational dynamics at the center of practice. When we refer to inquiry practice, we mean scientific and artistic explorations that advance knowledge and the co-construction of knowledge or learning. This definition applies as readily to what might occur in a classroom as what occurs among members of research team or a dance troupe.

Interdisciplinary Collaboration: Alternative Forms and Analytical Frames

Our goal in employing sociocultural learning theories as a lens for exploring various dimensions of collaborative faculty work is to identify practices that promote effective interdisciplinary collaboration and faculty (and student) learning and contexts that encourage or impede it. Research provides some insights into these concerns, but there is much more to learn. Our strategy is to use case studies as a source of information about discursive practices and interpersonal and institutional contexts that facilitate or impede interdisciplinary collaboration.

Much of the literature on interdisciplinarity is descriptive and prescriptive; observers typically recommend structures, policies, and practices that are believed to facilitate interdisciplinary work, but their suggestions are based on personal knowledge and experience rather than systematic study (Klein, 1990; Lattuca, 2001; Rhoten, 2003).

A significant limitation of many empirical studies on interdisciplinarity stems from the choice of subject to study. In the earliest studies, scholars interested in problem-based research and research management studied interdisciplinary research teams, typically composed of individuals trained in the natural and physical sciences, in both industry and academic settings. Occasionally these teams included social scientists, but scholars from the humanities, who are much less likely to engage in collaborative scholarship, were conspicuously absent. Research findings therefore were often limited in terms of applicability to different modes of scholarship, not just in terms of disciplines, but in terms of the types of scholarship. Researchers largely ignored interdisciplinary teaching and outreach activities.

More recently, scholars have identified a greater variety of approaches to interdisciplinary scholarship, including interdisciplinary projects in the social sciences and humanities, solo interdisciplinary research and teaching endeavors, and interdisciplinary projects influenced by postmodernism, feminism, and critical theory that do not rely on or seek to produce discipline-based knowledge (see Klein, 1996; Salter and Hearn, 1996; Lattuca, 2001).

Contexts for Interdisciplinary Work. A recurring theme in the literature on interdisciplinarity is its status in the discipline-oriented structure of the university. Often writers portray academic departments as hostile, or at best indifferent, to interdisciplinary research and teaching (Birnbaum, 1981; Klein, 1990; Hurst, 1992). Other impediments are passive research management policies that do not encourage or facilitate or direct interdisciplinary scholarship (Saxberg, Newell, and Mar, 1981); issues concerning indirect cost recovery distribution (Feller, 2002); financial resources that are restricted or uncertain (Epton, Payne, and Pearson, 1983); difficulties in accounting for activities and outputs that span academic units (Feller, 2002); and policies on faculty workload that discourage team teaching (Davis, 1995).

Weingart and Stehr (2000) noted that a paradoxical discourse surrounds interdisciplinarity: interdisciplinarity is viewed as an innovative form of knowledge production for which disciplinary knowledge is often viewed as a prerequisite. It is no wonder then that the university reward system is among the most often cited barriers to interdisciplinarity. Promotion, tenure, and salary decisions are determined in large measure by faculty who have been educated in specific disciplines and hold allegiances to academic departments. Untenured faculty may therefore fear repercussions from interdisciplinary scholarship, which brings potential loss of visibility and consequent lack of support for promotion (Gumport, 1993).

The real impediment to interdisciplinarity is not academic departments but the attitudes, beliefs, and values of gatekeepers, such as editorial board members and reviewers who police disciplinary boundaries. Clark (1983) and Becher (1989) contend that the discipline is the dominant force and the central source of identity for faculty members. Although disciplinary communities are not monolithic, they tend to espouse particular values and norms pertaining to scholarship.

Faculty members' decisions about research agendas and methods, however, are often based on personal commitments. Blackburn and Lawrence

(1995) found considerable support for a motivation-based framework for faculty work, which contends that faculty do what they think they are good at doing, devote energy to those things that interest them, and engage in activities in which they believe they can influence outcomes. Blackburn and Lawrence did not argue that institutional contexts were inconsequential; rather they claimed that social supports, such as departmental and institutional climates, can reinforce individuals' decisions to pursue particular pedagogical or inquiry strategies. Academic values such as collegiality and academic freedom may also influence collegial tolerance for different forms of academic work (Ruscio, 1987), such as interdisciplinarity.

How researchers conceptualize context in studies of interdisciplinarity is critical. The sociocultural theories that we rely on in this volume define contexts as multidimensional and complex. The term *context* refers not only to microcontexts, such as teaching teams or research collaborations, but to interpersonal contexts, such as local scholarly communities (including departments and schools), and extends to social and cultural contexts beyond the walls of colleges and universities. These contexts, of course, are overlapping and mutually influential, and they form constellations that affect the work of faculty members.

Understandings of context in sociological and anthropological studies of academic activity are generally consistent with a sociocultural perspective in which context is a multidimensional concept. Examples include Latour and Woolgar's well-known study of research activities at the Salk Institute (1979), studies of mission-oriented interdisciplinary ("big science") projects (Galison and Helvy, 1992), Scerri's study (2000) of interdisciplinary research at the Beckman Institute at California Institute of Technology, and Salter and Hearn's collection of personal accounts of interdisciplinarity in the social sciences and humanities (1996).

With an expanded view of context, researchers can explore how institutional and departmental policies, practices, and climates can both facilitate and hinder interdisciplinary work, sometimes simultaneously as practices in one arena come into conflict with practices from another. However, it is too easy to reify the obstacles created by departmental structures and overlook institutional policies that permit cross-departmental sharing of resources that, intentionally or not, support interdisciplinary collaboration. From a sociocultural standpoint, understanding the interaction of the various contexts that provide the test bed for particular interdisciplinary projects is critical to understanding why the teaching, research, or service activity is shaped in a particular way, how it develops (or stalls), and what is ultimately achieved.

Interdisciplinary Processes. Early studies of interdisciplinarity were typically less concerned with understanding the nature of interdisciplinary processes than with identifying which processes led to successful outcomes, which were typically defined as the integration of disciplinary perspectives (a presumed marker of interdisciplinarity). More recently, researchers have focused on the complex nature of interdisciplinary processes and tried to capture the interactions and working practices of individuals engaged in interdisciplinary projects (Creamer, 2003, 2004; Lattuca, 2001, 2002; Rhoten, 2003).

In an issue of *Ecosystems,* contributors noted that emerging interdisciplinary research often requires inductive approaches because there are no established theoretical frameworks to guide research (Pickett, Burch, and Grove, 1999; Redman, 1999; Turner and Carpenter, 1999). The complications that ensue not only from the absence of such guidelines in general, but from the challenge of combining different disciplinary—and sometimes epistemological—perspectives underlies most investigations of interdisciplinary collaborations.

Interpersonal dynamics among collaborators are a potential source of problems (Heberlein, 1988). Interpersonal conflict, however, when it stems from substantive rather than personal incompatibilities, can be a catalyst. Based on her studies of collaboration among faculty, Creamer (2004) proposes that innovations may be more likely when there is genuine engagement with differences of opinion regarding epistemological, methodological, or other substantive concerns among collaborators.

Recent studies of interdisciplinarity suggest that the act of sharing information (part of what we might term learning) is valuable in itself (Rhoten, 2003; Lattuca, 2001, 2002). Although knowledge production (particularly as measured by tangible outputs such as journal articles and research reports) is typically considered evidence of success, participants in interdisciplinary collaborations also value the opportunity to learn something about other disciplines, particularly when these disciplinary ways of knowing speak to their own preferred methods of doing research. For interdisciplinary collaborators, the intellectual benefits of talking across boundaries are as important as (and perhaps more important than) the traditional rewards associated with academic work.

Only a few studies offer insights into what might happen to faculty who teach interdisciplinary courses. In a study of interdisciplinary general education courses, Thorburn (1985) reported that participating faculty felt intellectually stimulated and claimed to have gained new teaching strategies, that is, they learned some things. Lattuca (2001) found that faculty engaged in interdisciplinary teaching, especially team teaching, were particularly reflective about their learning, as well as that of their students, as a result of that experience.

Petrie (1986) suggested that in order to work successfully on an interdisciplinary team, collaborating faculty had to learn something about the cognitive maps of their collaborators, at least their ways of looking at and interpreting phenomena and concepts. It seems likely that faculty cannot avoid how these ways intersect with their own ways of thinking. Newell (1994) claimed that these kinds of encounters in interdisciplinary courses could improve students' abilities to evaluate experts' testimony, increase their sensitivity to ethical issues and biases, and exercise their listening and creative thinking skills. Perhaps faculty who teach interdisciplinary courses experience similar kinds of learning as a result of interactions with subject matters and perspectives different than their own.

New Perspectives on Faculty Work

As calls for both collaboration (Austin, 2003; Brady, 1999; Rice, 1996) and interdisciplinarity (Boyer, 1990; Hackett, 2000; Rhoten, 2003) increase in colleges, universities, and the workplace, those who support, practice, and study faculty work need greater understanding of the nature and conduct of collaborative interdisciplinary work. The conceptual framework for this volume, which posits that much of faculty work can be understood as learning, provides an innovative perspective for examining accounts of different types of collaborative faculty activities in teaching, research, and service and outreach.

References

Austin, A. E. "Creating a Bridge to the Future: Preparing New Faculty for Face Changing Expectations in a Shifting Context." *Review of Higher Education*, 2003, 26(2), 119–144.

Becher, T. *Academic Tribes and Territories: Intellectual Enquiry and the Cultures of Disciplines*. Bristol, Pa.: Society for Research into Higher Education and Open University Press, 1989.

Birnbaum, P. H. "Academic Interdisciplinary Research: Characteristics of Successful Projects." *Academy of Management Journal*, 1981, 24, 487–503.

Blackburn, R. T., and Lawrence, J. H. *Faculty at Work: Motivation, Expectation, Satisfaction*. Baltimore, Md.: Johns Hopkins University Press, 1995.

Boyer, E. L. *Scholarship Reconsidered: Priorities of the Professoriate*. Princeton, N.J.: Carnegie Foundation for the Advancement of Teaching, 1990.

Brady, S. M. "Students at the Center of Education: A Collaborative Effort." *Liberal Education*, 1999, 85(1), 14–21.

Clark, B. R. *The Higher Education System: Academic Organization in Cross-National Perspective*. Berkeley: University of California Press, 1983.

Creamer, E. G. "Exploring the Link Between Inquiry Paradigm and the Process of Collaboration." *Review of Higher Education*, 2003, 26(4), 447–465.

Creamer, E. G. "Collaborators' Attitudes About Differences of Opinion." *Journal of Higher Education*, 2004, 75, 556–571.

Davis, J. R. *Interdisciplinary Courses and Team Teaching: New Arrangements for Learning*. Phoenix, Ariz.: American Council on Education and Oryx Press, 1995.

Epton, S. R., Payne, R. L., and Pearson, A. W. (eds.). *Managing Interdisciplinary Research*. New York: Wiley, 1983.

Feller, I. "New Organizations, Old Cultures: Strategy and Implementation of Interdisciplinary Programs." Paper presented at the American Association for the Advancement of Science Annual Meeting, Boston, Feb. 2002.

Galison, P., and Helvy, B. *Big Science*. Stanford, Calif.: Stanford University Press, 1992.

Gumport, P. A. "The Contested Terrain of Academic Program Reduction." *Journal of Higher Education,* 1993, *64*(3), 283–311.

Hackett, E. J. "Interdisciplinary Research Initiatives at the U.S. National Science Foundation." In P. Weingart and I. Stehr (eds.), *Practicing Interdisciplinarity.* Toronto: University of Toronto, 2000.

Heberlein, T. A. "Improving Interdisciplinary Research: Integrating the Social and Natural Sciences." *Society and Natural Resources,* 1999, *1,* 5–16.

Hurst, P. J. "The Research University as an Organizational Context for Collaboration: Cross-Departmental Research Collaboration in Environmental Studies." Unpublished doctoral dissertation, University of Michigan, 1992.

Klein, J. T. *Interdisciplinarity: History, Theory, and Practice.* Detroit, Mich.: Wayne State University Press, 1990.

Klein, J. T. *Crossing Boundaries: Knowledge, Disciplinarities, and Interdisciplinarities.* Charlottesville: University Press of Virginia, 1996.

Latour, B., and Woolgar, S. *Laboratory Life: The Construction of Scientific Facts.* Princeton, N.J.: Princeton University Press, 1979.

Lattuca, L. R. *Creating Interdisciplinarity: Interdisciplinary Research and Teaching Among College and University Faculty.* Nashville, Tenn.: Vanderbilt University Press, 2001.

Lattuca, L. R. "Learning Interdisciplinarity: Sociocultural Perspectives on Faculty Work." *Journal of Higher Education,* 2002, *73*(6), 711–739.

Newell, W. T. "Designing Interdisciplinary Courses." In J. T. Klein and W. Doty (eds.), *Interdisciplinary Studies Today.* San Francisco: Jossey-Bass, 1994.

Organisation for Economic Cooperation and Development. *Interdisciplinarity: Problems of Teaching and Research in Universities.* Paris: Organisation for Economic Cooperation and Development, 1972.

Petrie, H. G. "Do You See What I See? The Epistemology of Interdisciplinary Inquiry." In D. E. Chubin, A. L. Porter, F. A. Rossini, and T. Connelly (eds.), *Interdisciplinary Analysis and Research: Theory and Practice of Problem-Focused Research and Development.* Mt. Airy, Md.: Lomond, 1986.

Pickett, S.T.A., Burch, Jr., W. R., and Grove, J. M. "Interdisciplinary Research: Maintaining the Constructive Impulse in a Culture of Criticism." *Ecosystems,* 1999, *2*(1), 302–307.

Redman, C. L. "Human Dimensions of Ecosystem Studies." *Ecosystems,* 1999, *2*(1), 296–298.

Rhoten, D. *A Multi-Method Analysis of the Social and Technical Conditions for Interdisciplinary Collaboration.* San Francisco: Hybrid Vigor Institute, 2003.

Rice, R. E. *Making a Place for the New American Scholar.* Washington, D.C.: American Association for Higher Education, 1996.

Ruscio, K. P. "Many Sectors, Many Professions." In B. R. Clark (ed.), *The Academic Profession: National, Disciplinary, and Institutional Settings.* Berkeley: University of California Press, 1987.

Salter, L., and Hearn, A. *Outside the Lines: Issues in Interdisciplinary Research.* Montreal and Kingston, Canada: McGill-Queen's University Press, 1996.

Saxberg, B. O., Newell, W. T., and Mar, B. W. "Interdisciplinary Research—A Dilemma for University Central Administration." *SRA, Journal of the Society of Research Administrators,* 1981, *13,* 25–43.

Scerri, E. R. "Interdisciplinary Research at the Caltech Beckman Institute." In P. Weingart and I. Stehr (eds.), *Practising Interdisciplinarity.* Toronto: University of Toronto, 2000.

Thorburn, S. M. "Faculty Development Opportunities in Interdisciplinary General Education Programs." Unpublished doctoral dissertation, University of Maryland, 1985.

Turner, M. G., and Carpenter, S. R. "Tips and Traps in Interdisciplinary Research." *Ecosystems,* 1999, 2(1), 275–276.

Weingart, P., and Stehr, N. (eds.). *Practising Interdisciplinarity.* Toronto: University of Toronto, 2000.

LISA R. LATTUCA *is assistant professor and research associate in the Center for the Study of Higher Education at Pennsylvania State University in University Park, Pennsylvania.*

ELIZABETH G. CREAMER *is associate professor of educational research and evaluation in the Department of Educational Research and Policy Studies at Virginia Tech in Blacksburg, Virginia.*

2

Sociocultural and cultural-historical theories urge us to study the social relations and interactions of faculty embedded in local and particular contexts. They promise deeper insights into the work of college and university faculty.

Faculty Work as Learning: Insights from Theories of Cognition

Lisa R. Lattuca

Collaboration may be defined simply as an activity that involves individuals working together toward some agreed-on end. While there are many kinds of faculty collaboration, I will ground this discussion by referring to a study in which I explored the work of thirty-eight college and university faculty members who were engaged in interdisciplinary teaching and research (Lattuca, 2001). Regardless of their discipline, their institution, or their purposes (for example, teaching an interdisciplinary course or answering a research question), the majority of the faculty I interviewed talked about the learning required in their interdisciplinary collaborations. They often remarked on how much time they needed to learn new subject matter or new techniques critical to that work.

What did faculty learn from these forays into interdisciplinarity? Many described how they overcame discipline-based differences in language by attaining varying levels of fluency in other disciplinary languages. They learned new ways of conceptualizing phenomena or enhanced their understandings of new methods of inquiry. For some, new conceptualizations and modes of inquiry expanded or complemented their existing practices or beliefs and connected them with new scholarly communities. For a few, interdisciplinarity posed a considerable challenge to their discipline-based beliefs. In these cases, individuals reflected on the implications of what they had learned for their professional identities and epistemological commitments. These faculty members wondered if they still fit in their home disciplines when their scholarship challenged its borders and conventions.

NEW DIRECTIONS FOR TEACHING AND LEARNING, no. 102, Summer 2005 © Wiley Periodicals, Inc.

Other kinds of learning also occurred in interdisciplinary collaborations. Many faculty informants learned how to collaborate with individuals or groups of individuals with different ways of thinking about the same phenomena. Consider the case of a pair of faculty members team-teaching an interdisciplinary course for the first time. In preparing for and teaching the course, they will, even if unintentionally, learn how the other thinks about what students know, how the course should be taught, what should be assessed, and what counts as success. They must come to some level of consensus on these kinds of questions in order to work together effectively. The same kinds of learning may occur in research or service collaborations as faculty figure out their collaborators' strengths and weaknesses, likes and dislikes, and how to divide work to capitalize or avoid these.

In interdisciplinary collaborations, faculty may be more aware of their learning because they cannot take much for granted; their collaborators do not necessarily share the same knowledge base, methodological training or predilections, or even the same assumptions about knowledge itself. They may spend more time in discussion and reflection than collaborators who share a discipline in order to ensure that they agree on the essentials—or that they can disagree but still accomplish their goals.

This discussion of faculty learning in interdisciplinary collaborations is meant to confirm what many in higher education already know: faculty members in general do not stop learning once they have earned a terminal degree, but continue to learn throughout their academic careers. The interdisciplinary collaborators in my study were inspired (or required) to undertake significant learning activities to pursue their work, but learning is not limited to interdisciplinary collaborations or efforts. Discipline-based faculty also must keep up with advances in their areas of expertise, and their collaborative activities may be as likely to produce new learning as those of interdisciplinary collaborators.

Anna Neumann, a contributor to this volume, has been a leader in efforts to highlight the role of learning in faculty members' lives. In a series of studies she has explored the role of learning in scholarly identity development, subject matter expertise, and teaching (Neumann, 1992, 1995, 2000; Neumann and Peterson, 1997). Research on the role of learning in faculty members' lives is critical because the success of faculty members' learning experiences has real consequences for students, scholarly communities, and the larger society that is informed by their work. If learning is a prerequisite to teaching, research, and service, then higher education researchers and practitioners would be wise to understand the factors and contexts that promote and sustain faculty learning.

Studies often point to faculty development opportunities as key mechanisms for maintaining faculty productivity and satisfaction, but as Neumann (2000) noted, they "rarely position professions as potential sources of their own professional development" (p. 2). My own research on interdisciplinary teaching and research has clearly revealed the self-directed nature of faculty learning. Regardless of discipline, faculty described a similar process: they identified a topic they wanted to study, acknowledged that they did not have the necessary knowledge or methodological tools for the exploration they wanted to pursue, and eventually ascertained how they would go about answering the question they had posed. This description portrays learning as an individual activity. And often, in the early stages of conceptualizing a new project, faculty members appeared to be working alone. They read books and journals, used library and Internet resources, and occasionally attended a conference on the topic they wanted to learn more about. Yet however solitary these activities seem, they are nonetheless a form of social interaction: as faculty engage particular bodies of knowledge and methods of inquiry, they are using a set of cultural tools that have distinct social histories and uses. Rather than learning alone, they are learning in the company of those who have gone before them.

Here I see a great advantage in exploring interdisciplinary teaching and research as a form of faculty work: it forces us to think about the origins of the academic's cultural tools. The need to study interdisciplinarity presses the researcher to consider how the particular practices and tools of distinctive disciplinary (or interdisciplinary) communities shape faculty members' understandings of their work.

Disciplinary communities of practice are but one of the contexts that influence faculty work. Institutional values and norms may also shape the ways in which faculty work, although the salience of these institutional factors may vary depending on the type of institution (Austin, 2003). Consider, for example, how the research university ethos persuades faculty to value research activity over teaching and how these priorities might be reversed in a small liberal arts college. Social, economic, political, and cultural contexts also leave their mark on what individuals think about and how they think about it; recent explorations of race and gender have changed the nature of inquiry in fields like women's and ethnic studies, and have expanded the range of problems considered worth studying in the disciplines.

Our focus on interdisciplinary collaboration also makes clear that while learning is never really done in isolation, some kinds of faculty work are more overtly social in nature. They also provide an opportunity to study learning in situ, and the subsequent chapters reveal the processes that faculty craft in order to work together.

Once we include the role of the social and cultural (whether at the level of the classroom, the collaborative team, the academic department, the national context, or sociohistorical time), we come closer to describing understanding learning holistically. This is the important contribution made by sociocultural theories of learning, which highlight the intersubjective, social, cultural, and historical dimensions of what we learn, how we learn it, and why we learn it.

Learning as a Social and Cultural Activity

Educators are accustomed to thinking about cognition as an individual activity that occurs in one head at a time. This approach suggests that ways of thinking and learning are largely independent of, and unaffected by, the multilayered environments in which they occur and that cognition and learning are everywhere the same. Sociocultural theories challenge these assumptions and underscore the ways in which social interactions and social contexts shape learning.

A number of theories highlight the social and contextualized nature of learning (Lave, 1988; Lave and Wenger, 1991; Forman, Minick, and Stone, 1993; Rogoff, 1990; Greeno, 1997). Whether they are referred to as situated cognition, situated learning, activity theory, sociocultural, or cultural-historical theories, these proposals all rest on the claim that learning cannot be understood apart from its historical, cultural, and institutional contexts. (I use the shorthand term *sociocultural theory* to represent all of the perspectives just listed.) Because these theories cast learning as a fundamentally social and cultural activity, they contrast, often sharply, with behavioral and cognitive models that portray learning as an individual activity and as an artifact that can be easily separated from the contexts in which it takes place.

Sociocultural theories have their intellectual origins in the sociohistorical school of psychology developed by Lev Vygotsky and his colleagues. Vygotsky argued that in order to understand the individual, one must first understand the social context in which the individual exists (Wertsch, 1985). A complete explanation of learning therefore requires examination of the individual's own mental processes and the relevant social settings. This multidimensional analytical approach laid the groundwork for a dialectical model of learning in which individual and context interact in critical ways.

By shifting the unit of analysis from the individual to the sociocultural setting in which learning is embedded, theorists and researchers focus on the structures and interrelations within communities of practice. The result is a multifocal approach in which the individual and the context must be studied simultaneously.

Linkages Between Sociocultural and Cultural-Historical Theories

Both sociocultural theorists and activity theorists conceptualize human behavior and cognition as embedded in collectively organized, artifact-mediated systems. Mediating artifacts are the cultural tools and signs that allow us to communicate with one another. The texts that we read and the languages that we use to express ourselves, including mathematical and computer languages, as well as maps, diagrams, and works of art, are all examples of cultural tools. Tools and signs are described as mediating artifacts because they come between us and our objects, thus mediating our experience of the world (Wertsch, Del Rio, and Alvarez, 1995).

Cultural tools (also referred to as mediational means) shape the ways in which we interact with the world. These tools are developed and used by individuals and groups for different purposes, that is, they are the products of sociocultural evolution. We appropriate them so that we may participate in the particular social practices of our local communities and global society. These tools shape our actions but can also be adapted for unique purposes. For example, an academic discipline is an example of a cultural tool. Like other cultural tools, disciplines and fields frame the thinking and intellectual activity of individuals who are trained to use (or who decide to adopt) them.

Cultural tools do not merely facilitate actions that would ordinarily occur; they can alter "the entire flow and structure of mental functions" (Wertsch, Del Rio, and Alvarez, 1995, p. 23). Such a transformation allows new forms of mediated action to occur. One example of disciplinary transformation can be found in the often repeated definition of interdisciplinarity as borrowing (Klein, 1990): a scholar appropriates (borrows) the cultural tools of another discipline in order to study a phenomenon that could not be studied as well using the tools of her home discipline. But more than borrowing is in play. Wertsch (1985) and other sociocultural theorists would argue that adoption transforms the borrowed disciplinary concepts, perspectives, or methods so that they may be used in the service of learning in a different field or discipline. Transformation occurs as the tools are put to new uses and, often, as they are purposefully altered for use in the new field.

Most sociocultural theorists view mediation broadly, often focusing on the critical role that others, particularly the more skilled members of a community of practice, play in mediating the learning of others. The classroom teacher is a prime example of the skilled mediator, but others may also serve this purpose. Apprenticeship is a vehicle for socializing new members of a community. Wertsch, Del Rio, and Alvarez (1995) contend that socialization can be "viewed largely in terms of how learners 'appropriate' the existing strategies of others and hence reproduce an existing cognitive and social order" (p. 16). By working together, the apprentice and the more skilled other develop "increasing intersubjectivity" (p. 16). Apprentices, of course, do not become carbon copies of their tutors or mentors, and apprenticeship should not be misconstrued purely as a process of reproduction. Learning in sociocultural theories is inherently constructivist and the learner is the agent who actively makes sense of the world.

How do effective learning and social practices emerge in a new community of practice? Is there a central form of participation that can be appropriated in such a situation? Can sociocultural and cultural-historical theories help us define when a group of individuals becomes a community of practice?

Sociocultural and cultural-historical theories offer assistance in answering these questions by insisting that researchers take a historical perspective on social practices. This perspective helps us see why certain social practices come to the fore in a new activity. A historical perspective also implies a developmental perspective (Engeström, 1999a). We can explore social practices, mediating artifacts, and the objects of our practices in terms of how they develop and change. We can explore moments of internalization of social practices when individuals learn and appropriate the habits of thinking and doing that characterize a community of practice (cultural historical theorists liken internalization to socialization). But we can also study periods of externalization, when there are disruptions and contradictions in accepted practices in a community or when community members subject their beliefs and activities to critique and reflection. If internalization allows us to work together within the box, externalization allows us to break out of the box, enabling groups and individuals to learn new things, imagine new forms of practice, and avoid endlessly repeating what has been done before. Would we better understand the work of the collaborators in the cases that follow in Chapters Three through Five if we explore how cycles of internalization and externalization contribute to the smooth functioning of groups, as well as to breakthroughs in practices that allow collaborations to advance their work?

Activity theorists argue that social practices are oriented toward particular objects. The symposium from which this volume grew is an example of such an activity—in this case, a discussion of theoretical perspectives on faculty work. This form of academic exchange (the conference symposium) is itself a social practice that has been influenced by the history and culture of academic professional organizations. This symposium was also shaped by the concerns of the organization that sponsored it, the researchers who proposed it, and the audience that participated in it (and perhaps other cultural contexts as well). Each of these contexts is immersed in, and influenced by, specific cultural and historical moments. Lest this seem too determinative, sociocultural theories hasten to add that social practices are mutually constitutive: individuals can internalize as well as externalize practices. We can act according to the status quo or can generate new practices that better suit our evolving communities.

To continue the illustration of sociocultural and cultural-historical theories through the example of this volume, we can define the object of our activity as the exploration of new ways of studying and understanding faculty work. Activity theorists warn us not to confuse objects with goals. Goals, Engeström (1999b) contends, are attached to specific actions. Relying on Weick (1995), Engeström argues that goals are formulated and revised as groups act. They are often explicated clearly only when they are achieved. In contrast, objects are more like horizons for which we reach. The following example may make this abstraction more concrete. Using the example of our volume once again, I suggest that we should not conceptualize the task of advancing research on faculty work as a clear and finite task to be completed in a given time frame. Rather, we should understand our goal of enhancing the theory base for research on faculty work as an ongoing dialogue. This dialogue has no particular end point; with every advance, we are likely to think of new issues to consider and new problems to be solved. It may be only when we have nearly accomplished our task that we will best understand what it was we were truly after.

Engeström's identification of moments of internalization and externalization highlight socioculturalists' warnings that increasing intersubjectivity does not guarantee mutual understanding and can instead produce divergent perspectives, opposing ideas, resistance, and other forms of disharmony. Smolka, De Goes, and Pino (1995) suggest that rather than searching for symmetry or harmony in social relations, we should explore "reciprocal processes": "Reciprocity does not, however, have the same harmonious meaning as 'mutuality,' which pervades the notion of Intersubjectivity. Here, 'reciprocal' is used in the sense of being inversely related, as the empowering of one subject disempowers the other. But yet, in a deeper sense, we can say that 'reciprocal' means 'constitutively related'" (p. 178). One need only to think about the potential for controversy in advancing new approaches to the study of faculty work to understand that the construction of the object of an activity is not necessarily harmonious. Rather, the act of constructing an object—in this case, improved research practice in higher education—is a collaborative and dialogical process in which, Engeström (1999b) notes, "different perspectives and voices meet, collide, and merge" (p. 382). These different perspectives are rooted in different communities and in different practices that can continue to coexist within a collective activity system. According to Engestrom, a shared understanding of a problem or object is a collaborative and analytical achievement because shared understanding of a problem or task can rarely be taken for granted. In fact, he argues that the task of problem construction is crucial to innovative learning and social practice.

Implications for Research on Faculty Work

The theoretical perspective of sociocultural theories is profoundly contextual, that is, they orient us toward the influence and development of historically situated practices. To build this kind of understanding of academic practices—whether these are classified as outreach, teaching, research, or some combination of the three—we need an expansive conception of the word *context* that goes beyond the typical attention paid in higher education studies to institutional type, discipline, location, selectivity, or other commonly used variables that focus on macro-level traits of communities rather than the micro-level social practices that characterize, and often distinguish, them.

We know, for example, that disciplinary communities not only share values and norms but at times contest these values and norms. Faculty members espouse methods but also challenge them. While it is useful to acknowledge the role of discipline in helping us to identify typical ways of thinking and working, we also recognize that individuals within disciplines represent unique constellations of theoretical choices, epistemological commitments, and beliefs about what is important to study and how to study it. To understand whether a particular interdisciplinary faculty collaboration is successful, we have to parse the individual understandings of the disciplines that are involved at a given time. How do members of the collaboration view their home disciplines? How do they view and understand the disciplines of others engaged in the collaboration? How do the social practices of each collaborator reflect, or reject, disciplinary preferences? How do the members of the collaboration view the object of their collaboration (practice), the tools (mediating artifacts) they bring to the collaborative work, and the forms and qualities of the social interactions and organization they develop? This is the expanded understanding of context that is required in a study that takes the social and cultural nature of learning and activity seriously.

This expanded notion of context allows us to conceptualize faculty learning and activity as embedded in a variety of intersecting contexts. Faculty learning and work may take place in the immediate setting of the laboratory or office, but those settings are situated within the social practices of particular departments, institutions, and academic disciplines and in particular moments in time. By tracing the influence of the social practices of both local and larger communities, we will better understand how and what people learn and do. We can explore how competing contexts reify or bury new ideas, how converging schools of thought can facilitate the creation of new knowledge, how breakthroughs are catalyzed by existing conditions, and how deeply embedded beliefs can stifle creative moves that are resurrected later when the conditions for their acceptance prevail. Because sociocultural theories are committed to explicating contexts—temporal, immediate, and more distal—they require in-depth exploration of the multiple contexts in which faculty work is embedded. To fully understand any particular context, we must think in terms of how that context intersects with other contexts in which faculty work (think, for example, of the overlapping but potentially competing cultures of departments and institutions). We must also think historically about why particular contexts developed in particular ways, why they intersect as they do, and how they influence the activity of those working within them.

Sociocultural and cultural-historical theories urge us to study the social relations and interactions of faculty embedded in local and particular contexts. Their promise is deeper insight into the work of college and university faculty.

References

Austin, A. E. "Creating a Bridge to the Future: Preparing New Faculty for Face Changing Expectations in a Shifting Context." *Review of Higher Education*, 2003, 26(2), 119–144.

Engeström, Y. "Activity Theory and Individual and Social Transformation." In Y. Engeström, R. Meittinen, and R.-J. Punamaki (eds.), *Perspectives on Activity Theory.* Cambridge: Cambridge University Press, 1999a.

Engeström, Y. "Innovative Learning in Work Teams: Analyzing Cycles of Knowledge Creation in Practice." In Y. Engeström, R. Meittinen, and R.-J. Punamaki (eds.), *Perspectives on Activity Theory.* Cambridge: Cambridge University Press, 1999b.

Forman, E. A., Minick, N, and Stone, C. A. *Contexts for Learning: Sociocultural Dynamics in Children's Development.* New York: Oxford University Press, 1993.

Greeno, J. G. "On Claims That Answer the Wrong Question." *Educational Researcher,* 1997, 26(1), 5–17.

Klein, J. T. *Interdisciplinarity: History, Theory, and Practice.* Detroit, Mich.: Wayne State University Press, 1990.

Lattuca, L. R. *Creating Interdisciplinarity: Interdisciplinary Research and Teaching Among College and University Faculty.* Nashville, Tenn.: Vanderbilt University Press, 2001.

Lave, J. *Cognition in Practice: Mind, Mathematics and Culture in Everyday Life.* Cambridge: Cambridge University Press, 1988.

Lave, J., and Wenger, E. *Situated Learning: Legitimate Peripheral Participation.* New York: Cambridge University Press, 1991.

Neumann, A. "Colleges Under Pressure: Budgeting, Presidential Competence, and Faculty Uncertainty." *Leadership Quarterly,* 1992, 3(3), 191–215.

Neumann, A. "Context, Cognition, and Culture: A Case Analysis of Collegiate Leadership and Cultural Change." *American Educational Research Journal,* 1995, 32(2), 251–279.

Neumann, A. "Toward a Profession of Learning: Exploring How University Professors Learn Their Subjects Through Teaching." Paper presented at the annual meeting of the American Educational Research Association, New Orleans, Apr. 2000.

Neumann, A., and Peterson, P. L. *Learning from Our Lives: Women, Research, and Autobiography in Education.* New York: Teachers College Press, 1997.

Rogoff, B. *Apprenticeship in Thinking: Cognitive Development in Social Context.* New York: Oxford University Press, 1990.

Smolka, A.L.B., De Goes, M.C.R., and Pino A. "The Constitution of the Subject: A Persistent Question." In J. V. Wertsch, P. Del Rio, and A. Alvarez (eds.), *Sociocultural Studies of Mind.* Cambridge: Cambridge University Press, 1995.

Weick, K. E. *Sense-Making in Organizations.* Thousand Oaks, Calif.: Sage, 1995.

Wertsch, J. V. *Vygotsky and the Social Formation of Mind.* Cambridge, Mass.: Harvard University Press, 1985.

Wertsch, J. V., Del Rio, P., and Alvarez, A. (eds.). *Sociocultural Studies of Mind.* Cambridge: Cambridge University Press, 1995.

LISA R. LATTUCA is assistant professor and research associate in the Center for the Study of Higher Education at Pennsylvania State University in University Park, Pennsylvania.

The authors propose a model of the stages of interdisciplinary collaboration grounded in their experiences as external evaluators of a university-community partnership.

Interdisciplinary Collaboration and Academic Work: A Case Study of a University-Community Partnership

Marilyn J. Amey, Dennis F. Brown

The definition of collaboration represented in this chapter was initially envisioned by the project administrator of a group of educators we studied and simply was a bringing together of members from various fields to apply their expertise in successfully resolving complex problems. Unlike traditional faculty work, the intent was to have the faculty come together intellectually, not just functionally according to their institutional roles. What we saw emerge in the evolution of the group was that faculty came to think collectively in generating strategies that used the strengths of their individual disciplinary and paradigmatic expertise in a more genuinely integrated way. Members felt ownership for the group, its direction, and its decision making and felt accountability to each other. They were motivated by the collegial discourse and learning opportunities leading to the creation of new knowledge and understandings. The complex set of cognitively and structurally developmental interactions that emerged over the length of this project is what we called interdisciplinary collaboration.

The Case

The team represented in this case was involved in an eighteen-month study of a university-community partnership. The purpose of the partnership project was to develop the community's capacity to operate a community center that would provide a wide range of services and respond to future needs. The ten-member university team was contracted by a state social services agency to provide technical assistance and training to an inner-city community council. The team members were faculty, staff, and graduate students from five units at one university: social welfare, urban affairs, museum studies, sociology, and university extension.

We examined the ways in which university team members developed and enacted an interdisciplinary team and the leadership issues associated with group cohesion. Several themes emerged from this analysis, and we eventually developed an interdisciplinary collaboration model to capture the complexity of the activity. Specifically, we examined the consequences of competing disciplinary assumptions for group processes, goal definition, and intervention strategies. We also explored leadership issues and the impact of university culture on successful interdisciplinary collaboration development.

Data collection for the case study included observations of team meetings, audiorecorded individual interviews with team members, analysis of project documents (minutes, memoranda, and reports), and analysis of reflective papers written by team members that highlighted important decision points and other perceptions of group processes.

Interdisciplinary Collaboration Model

Throughout their involvement with the project, group members learned to work together as a team, and the team learned to work in a very different kind of partnership process. Table 3.1 depicts a visual construction of the interdisciplinary collaboration model of team behavior we observed in this study. The dimensions of the model resemble findings from previous research by Tuckman (1965), Bolman and Deal (1997), and Bensimon and Neumann (1993). By portraying the complementary and simultaneous development of the team across multiple dimensions, our model presents a more complete and complex perspective than authors who focused on only one dimension. Three stages emerged that represent distinctive characteristics along the four dimensions of discipline orientation, knowledge engagement, work orientation, and leadership.

Discipline orientation refers to the disciplinary paradigm that guides how members view and interpret the environment and how they typically address solutions to problems in that environment. There are several approaches to cross-disciplinary work: dominant, when one paradigm dominates and provides direction and meaning for change; parallel, with paradigms positioned more equally, and different paradigms providing direction and meaning for distinct portions of work without one orientation framing the effort; and integrated, where multiple frameworks inform the process, blending together to form an interdisciplinary perspective. The hybrid or integrative side of the continuum represents a melding of philosophical thought and interdisciplinary learning.

Table 3.1. Interdisciplinary Collaboration Model

Dimensions	Stage One	Stage Two	Stage Three
Discipline orientation	Dominant	Parallel	Integrative
Knowledge engagement	Expert	Coordinated	Collaborative
Work orientation	Individual	Group	Team
Leadership	Top down	Facilitative, inclusive	Weblike, servant

Knowledge engagement refers to how members use disciplinary knowledge and the role they play within the group. The continuum of knowledge engagement begins with the expert model, moves to the coordinated approach, and finally evolves into a collaborative stage. Traditional outreach and consulting work are examples of the expert model of knowledge engagement where individuals are sought for their disciplinary expertise (Doan, 1995; O'Looney, 1994). As development occurs across the continuum, the expert moves to serve more as a learning facilitator, sharing the intellectual platform with various collaborators, including the clients, and promoting diverse perspectives.

Work orientation refers to how each member works with other group members. It begins with a focus on the individual and individual activity, moves through a group orientation, and finally evolves to a team functioning with collective responsibility for goal attainment.

Leadership, the fourth dimension of the model, refers to the behaviors of the person administratively responsible for group and meeting its contractual obligations. Transitions on the leadership dimension were characterized as top down, to facilitative and more inclusive, and finally, to weblike or servant. The stages are not time bound, but we believe they are developmental in nature. (See Amey and Brown, 2004, for further explanation of the model.)

Stage One: Dominant, Expert, Individual, Top Down. In Stage One, the group was preoccupied with the tasks of group formation, role and goal clarification, task allocation, and paradigm exploration. Members viewed project problems and intervention strategies through their own disciplinary lenses and behaved as though they alone had the answers. The group exchanged information but functioned and thought independently. As noted by two members, "[We each] basically just had one approach [to the job]" and "We were running our own agendas." The team was actually a collection of individuals positioning themselves and their disciplinary paradigms as dominant. As experts in particular knowledge domains inclined to work individually on tasks, they responded to the invitation to participate in the effort as they had in past consultancies:

> [We used] a traditional response—respond to a request from a customer— a consultancy. We were brought in so we treated this as a similar event. I

prepared the scope of work for the contract, laid out the tasks that needed
to take place. . . . My anticipation was that team members would be assigned
to deliver those tasks. [We were] basically supposed to provide specific work
to accomplish each task.

Leadership at this stage was traditional (top down) and leader centered
(Bennis, 1986) requiring visioning, decision making, and conflict resolution intervention up front and maintaining power and authority with the
leader. The designated leader and the member of the group with the most
senior status saw her role as administrative. This stage corresponds to the
traditional research-consultant approach to community interventions (Fear
and Sandmann, 1997). One member reflected, "At the beginning, it was a
jockeying for positions, actually. People didn't know each other around the
table. So who was in the group and why they are in the group and the identity of those people in the group needed to be developed, needed to be
shared. And there needed to be an increased appreciation for the background and expertise that people would bring that would make them legitimate members of the group."

Clashes were frequent throughout Stage One, as proponents for the two
primary disciplinary paradigms represented could not easily gain advantage
over the other. The conflicts often centered on how to work with the community and what form of training needed to be delivered in this project. For
example, members whose orientation to community work emphasized an
economic approach to community building were in staunch disagreement
with those operating from a perspective that emphasized building human
capacity. It took substantial time and effort before the proponents of either
paradigm realized its limitations in fulfilling the real needs of the community; both approaches had been independently used in community-based
projects, and both experienced failure in the long run.

Eventually the tension from the paradigm clashes caused the group
members to seek and construct a less stressful atmosphere that allowed
them to work on tasks together. The group looked for ways to depersonal-
ize the disciplinary debates, including talking in the third person, referring
to the community more frequently in discussions. They asked each other,
"What would the community want?" rather than leading with the more
politically charged and self-serving, "I think it would be best if . . . " In this
way, members could discuss issues without having first to attack another's
disciplinary orientation, thereby repositioning oneself as "expert." One illustration of this is through the group's incorporation of the term *guardianship*.
Apart from the university group, the community council adopted an
approach in their deliberations they termed "guardianship," which was not
an approach to community development inherent in the disciplinary cultures of any of the group members. To the council, *guardianship* meant their
collective responsibility to oversee and protect the assets of the community.
The university group slowly adopted and internalized this concept and used

it as the basis for establishing what we called the intellectual neutral space that eventually enabled the group to move beyond the shackles of their tightly held disciplinary lenses. "[Adopting guardianship] pulled us out of [any] one person's conceptual way of thinking or framework," offered a member.

The neutral space was constructed as members of the group internalized the concept and language of the others. During this phase as they metaphorically entered the neutral space, members spent more time listening than "reloading" and more time with inquiry than advocacy, which helped to establish trust and respect within the group. An intellectual neutral space seemed necessary for the multidisciplinary group to move from Stage One to Stage Two of our developmental model. It was a point at which the exploration of disciplinary paradigms and attempts at dialogue could really begin, thereby representing transition between the distinct and conflicting characteristics of Stage One and the coordinated and norming elements of Stage Two.

Stage Two: Parallel, Coordinated, Group, Facilitative. Stage Two was characterized by aspects of group norming (coming to agreement and understanding of certain goals and values), refining and coordinating work processes, leadership transition, and paradigm cohesion. Through accommodating the concepts and language of others, members maintained the intellectual neutral space to progress toward project goals, more connected work, and early stages of team development. This was an active, task-oriented period, and group members met more frequently than they had previously. Competing disciplinary perspectives existed in parallel, allowing tasks to be done independently and brought back to the group for coordination and compilation. Although members remained committed to their own disciplinary orientations, many began to acknowledge that other paradigms had merit in some situations. Trust and respect among group members grew as a sense of ownership of the process and product developed.

Individual voices were attended to as professional respect and acceptance slowly developed within the group. There was less paradigm competition, reflected in the comment of one participant: "We were looking to get more academic synergy, to have a campus group that met and shared experiences from multidisciplinary points of view and have an interchange between [the various disciplines]." As members began to feel collective responsibility for the intellectual processes of their work, including raising and synthesizing issues and monitoring values and behaviors, they showed signs of expressive teams that provide some mutual support and counsel to each other and to the leader (Bensimon and Neumann, 1993). This way of functioning created a sense of connectedness among group members for their joint work. They began to express opinions outside their areas of knowledge expertise and assigned tasks. More time was spent intellectually engaging with the subprojects on which others worked to offer thoughtful comment and constructive criticism, brainstorming next steps, and helping the project leader generate responses to outside constituents.

During this time, there was a leadership transition to a person already a member of the group who had a more facilitative and inclusive style. In describing his approach, the new leader expressed: "I think of myself as being responsible as an enabler in the project. By that, I mean being responsible for trying to see that the different points of view in the project are brought together and issues are identified and that they are resolved—to establish a structural process where other people can do their best work." While the approach to leadership changed with the new leader, whom we called the transition leader, final authority for decision making remained with his predecessor, the project administrator.

As is common in funded research projects, critical events continued to challenge the group during Stage Two. These tensions and conflicts often caused members to revisit the role they wanted to play in the group, their commitment to the length of the project, as well as the university's partnership role. In referencing some of these clashes, one person suggested, "There was just a lack of communication. . . . There was still a level of distrust of what the university might do with their relationship to the community." Each crisis caused the group members to seek the decision-making and conflict resolution authority of the project administrator, indicating that they were not yet fully ready for a facilitative or servant leader of the transition leader.

Stage Three: Integrative, Collaborative, Team, Weblike. It is difficult to provide a complete description of Stage Three because the case group did not fully reach this hypothesized stage. We believe this stage would be characterized by adaptation and integration of ideas and the development of collective cognition and shared understandings among team members. Disciplinary paradigms moved from competing (Stage One) through coexisting (Stage Two) to integrated in Stage Three.

Individual members did not replace their paradigmatic lenses with new ones but saw through adaptive lenses that recognized the contributions of once competing perspectives. In this sense, the paradigm evolution is developmental. In Stage Three, members do not compete for dominance for their disciplinary orientation, but look for ways in which cognitive perspectives complement each other and can be integrated into new understandings as problems are further defined and resolutions created. Communication, both formal and informal, increases as ideas are exchanged and recreated. Members of the team are motivated as much by the learning and by integrating multiple perspectives as they are by successfully completing their original mission. Through dialogue, new knowledge is created, and therefore new solutions are possible. From the team members' perspectives, this evolution represents fundamental change.

Active listening, reflection, and continuous learning are cornerstones of Stage Three. The team is highly adaptive in creating solutions and open to the free, uninhibited debate of issues. They have developed into a more self-governing and intellectually connected team, more in line with the concepts of cognitive teams expressed by Bensimon and Neumann (1993). The team assumes collective responsibility for the work, team maintenance, and development. These values and behaviors supplant the need for an authoritarian leadership model, as leadership can flow more freely through the team members based on the project needs.

Crises do not threaten the group and reopen old wounds but provide opportunities for the team to develop their collective cognition further. All members share responsibility for their actions and collective decisions. Members grow to trust and respect each other in the altruistic motivation and advancement of the team. As a result, the team is truly greater than the sum of its parts. In a sense, the group has evolved to an interdisciplinary team: disciplinary boundaries seem to disappear because they have become much less obvious and obstructionist, and new interdisciplinary perspectives, and new knowledge, are created.

Shared values are internalized, not merely intellectualized, and they guide the development of the team's cognitive lens. Through ongoing interaction and engagement with the ideas of others, members were deeply challenged along the knowledge engagement (ways of connecting to knowledge) and disciplinary orientation (lenses through which one views the world) continua. Their views were being informed, altered, and adapted by their interactions with others; they were learning. To develop a collective cognitive lens, each team member has to make conscious the mental models and disciplinary paradigms that often function below the level of awareness yet guide behavior and affect decision making (Kegan, 1982; Kuhnert and Lewis, 1989; Senge, 1990). Then each has to be willing and able to attend to, and later incorporate, the cultural filters, mental models, and disciplinary paradigms of others. One has to be willing and able to learn. This cognitive process and development leads to the integrative thinking we posited as central to achieving interdisciplinary collaboration. Although it was not fully realized by every member we studied, and therefore remains speculative, there was sufficient evidence of this kind of intellectual development by many members for us to define this third stage.

Mediating Artifacts and Tools

Sociocultural theories help us understand more clearly the role of discipline, graduate preparation, and reward systems that are primarily influenced by academic disciplines, institutional missions, and organizational cultures on faculty behavior in academic work.

Training and Rewards. It was clear in the early stages of this research that the university team behaved in accordance with familiar disciplinary and institutional norms to which they were socialized and for which they were rewarded by the university and by their disciplinary colleagues. Identification with the discipline begins with the socialization experiences of graduate school, during which students learn the language, style, symbols, values, traditions, and folklore of respective disciplines as well as appropriate professional activities for the field (Austin, 2002; Becher, 1989; Golde, 1998). They are trained to be experts on the cutting edge of increasingly specialized areas within their chosen discipline, especially if they are interested in research faculty careers. University and disciplinary reward systems, often based on a particularly narrow set of sanctioned behaviors, reinforce these graduate school socializations, keeping many faculty members organizing their work within narrow bands of perceived acceptability. Reward structures that are normed on individual contributions and the traditional academic cycle often do not accommodate collaborative scholarship, which often takes longer to produce. Credit for cross-disciplinary activity, multiple authorship, and the time required to disseminate findings in outlets atypical to the discipline become points of dissension for faculty participants as they confront their colleagues in annual evaluations and promotion reviews. Activities completed in conjunction with public agencies or communities, as for our case study faculty, are often couched in terms of service, not scholarship, and there again are devalued in the reward structure even though they provide excellent opportunities for interdisciplinary collaboration. Both graduate preparation and institutional and disciplinary reward structures seem to perpetuate Stage One behavior that we describe in our model.

If we are to truly foster the kind of Stage Three work we advocate, we need to more closely examine how we socialize students in graduate school and throughout their academic careers to work successfully in collaborative efforts. If these interdisciplinary efforts require a different set of skills and experiences in order to be successful, then this learning needs to occur, and be reinforced, before other Stage One thinking becomes deeply embedded and potentially unalterable. Involving students in collaborative and cross-disciplinary research projects, for example, provides opportunity to see the limitations of disciplinary perspectives in problem solving and idea generation, engage actively with other disciplinary perspectives in authentic ways, and reflect on and thereby perhaps integrate different knowledge perspectives into one's own thinking.

Changing faculty reward structures to support interdisciplinary collaboration is perhaps an even greater cultural change, in spite of decades of rhetoric to do so. Advocates of interdisciplinary academic work argue that it likely yields more innovative and consequential results for complex problems than traditional, individual research efforts (Klein, 1990; Salter and Hearn, 1996; Sandmann and Flynn, 1997) and that it therefore suggests assessment of scholarly impact rather than only volume. Inevitably at first, changing reward structures to look at impact results in a more labor-intensive evaluation process for faculty, because simply counting publications, presentations, and grant dollars will be insufficient. But without such differences in accounting for work, little change will occur. In many ways, interdisciplinary collaboration and a focus on impact leads to research for the public good (Fairweather, 1996).

Collective Work, Collaboration, and Cognitive Constructions. Collaborative efforts take time to be successful: time for the collaborative and dialogical process to unfold and time for a common understanding to be collectively constructed. When faculty work together on projects, it is far more likely to be either a hierarchical situation (for example, senior-junior mentoring relationship, senior researcher with research associate) or a doling out of responsibilities to be brought back to a senior analyst for compilation (what we called cooperation). In traditional relationships, for example, problem construction for the work is less often a collective activity but is assumed to be the responsibility of senior colleagues, knowledge experts, or the designated leader of the group. It is not the more authentic collaboration of intellectual peers where shared understanding underpins the activities referenced in sociocultural theory. Most of those who joined the project we studied expected it to take this more cooperative form that would allow them to work basically independently as knowledge experts and remain largely unaffected intellectually by the presence of others.

The approach proposed for this project, while not entirely successful in creating a truly interdisciplinary experience for all members, asked members to try to move beyond their personal research preferences and practice orientations and to explore the utility of interdisciplinary work and multi-method engagement and scholarship. For those who pursued their work in intellectual isolation, as they "had always done," the experience was often frustrating, limiting, and did not produce expected results based on past Stage One practices. As the project proceeded, the values for most members changed, and individual activity became less valued than collective thinking and action. For those willing to work beyond their intellectual training and spheres, there was evidence of some degree of synergy, generativity, and a sense of collective pride in the outcome.

If interdisciplinarity can be a kind of borrowing of cultural tools, and this appropriation is indeed a transformative action, we need to consider how we effectively create the space and time in faculty work to support this ongoing transformation. We believe that interdisciplinary collaboration is rooted in a dialogical method of inquiry that engages multiple parties in a joint search for knowledge and common understanding. Beyond transcending cultural and bureaucratic boundaries such as the reward structure and academic calendar, interdisciplinary collaboration requires cultivating dialogue, developing shared language and understandings, reflection, and deep learning—all attributes of adult learning (Mezirow, 1991) but not often principles promoted in academic life. There are no easy answers to how this occurs, just as interdisciplinary collaboration is not an easy process of intellectual development. Although this may be a cognitive process that happens simply as a function of faculty coming together to work on a project, our study leads us to believe that this kind of transformation is encouraged or facilitated by a leader who may be associated with but not as deeply embedded in the process, at least initially.

The Importance of the Leader. There were significant institutional challenges associated with the project we studied. One was bringing together the right persons who were in control of the right processes at the right time. Another was creating a management structure to support the team efforts. Both challenges required careful planning and adequate time for design, agreement, and negotiation. Most funded projects involving interdisciplinary collaboration do not allow much time after the award is made, and it is difficult to anticipate all the pitfalls and concerns in advance of an actual award. Our study showed that a leader who understands the institution's management workings, including the bureaucratic and reward structures, and who has effective administrative and negotiating skills is an important principal player.

Team development and interdisciplinary collaboration are experiments where process is as important as product: disciplinary distinctions need to be addressed, typical faculty identity issues reconciled, and relationship and behavioral norms established. All of these factors were part of the initial phases of the group's development, characterized as Stage One in our model. We believe they are typical of the way in which any interdisciplinary collaboration or intellectual team activity would unfold. Actively socializing people to the team, keeping them involved and their work interconnected, and dealing effectively with the varying range and style of interpersonal interactions are process factors that affect all kinds of collective work. Being aware of the potential need for and knowing how to interject or create the neutral space as well as understanding the interpersonal side of team development, especially when disciplinary boundaries need to be crossed, seems a valuable leadership process. All of this requires attention, regular communication, and ongoing maintenance. In some respects, these examples may be fairly common of any early team development struggles, and yet, especially in contractual situations like funded research and other kinds of outreach scholarship, sufficient time to develop the normative and cultural infrastructure to support team functioning is often minimized, if not eliminated altogether.

In this case, although it was not used very often or particularly cultivated as a leadership strategy, cultural leadership was important. A leader using a cultural approach to interdisciplinary collaboration and team development looks for ways to reinforce stories and myths, use jargon and create shared language, celebrate achievements, and ritualize activities so that members regularly feel a sense of connection to a greater whole (Bolman and Deal, 1997; Morgan, 1999; Tierney, 1991). In our study, when it occurred, finding ways to reinforce group goals, trying to develop common language, and leaving situations unresolved for strategic periods of time to build creative tension and interdependence within the group were examples of cultural leadership the project administrator used to facilitate developmental progress within the group. What was also clear was that there were many missed opportunities for providing the organizational theater (Bolman and Deal, 1997) to strengthen team functioning and enhance overall team development. Leaders must pay attention simultaneously to the three dimensions of growth and development (disciplinary orientation, knowledge engagement, and work orientation), which is a challenge but a necessity. These dimensions affect each other and may require different approaches to leadership and development over time.

As we realized in studying our research team, leading interdisciplinary collaboration efforts is about facilitating learning for the members of the group and for the leader. Vaill (1997, p. 4) calls this orientation the "learning premise" and suggests that being involved in a learning process or proceeding from a learning premise means to be "continually confronted with newness—new problems, ideas, techniques, concepts; new gestalts; new possibilities and new limits; new awareness and understandings of oneself." Learning also means reinterpreting things already understood and letting go of former understandings and techniques, even if one never literally "unlearns."

In a setting where both technical and intellectual skills are involved, leaders have to focus on helping faculty become active inquirers into their own and others' practices in order for this kind of learning to occur. Bartlett (1990) spoke to the same thing we portrayed in our discussion of the intellectual aspects of interdisciplinary collaboration when she wrote, "Because knowledge arises within social contexts and in multiple forms, the key to increasing knowledge lies in an effort to extend one's limited perspective [to learn]" (p. 882). Members need to recognize that their expertise is "special knowledge, but limited knowledge" and that they need to move beyond their own knowledge spheres "to understand other perspectives" (p. 882). This is done in part by acquiring new lenses for critically assessing team circumstances and members' role (including the leader) in determining these circumstances (Smyth, 1989).

Cultivating this kind of member cognitive development is an important aspect of leadership in interdisciplinary collaborations and requires of the leader the capacity to see things from multiple perspectives. Leaders need to be cognitively complex thinkers with skills in critical thinking, listening, and knowing how to learn (Amey, 2002). Bringing together integrated thinkers across multiple perspectives requires higher-order leadership skills than reflected in traditional, hierarchical group work. It need not be that the person with the title or the appointed leader is the only person who is facilitating these thinking processes, but without this form of leadership present throughout the group's time together, we believe there will not be transitions along the interdisciplinary collaboration model we propose.

References

Amey, M. J. "Evaluating Outreach Performance." In C. L. Colbeck (ed.), *Evaluating Faculty Performance.* New Directions for Institutional Research, no. 114. San Francisco: Jossey-Bass, 2002.

Amey, M. J., and Brown, D. F. *Breaking Out of the Box: Interdisciplinary Collaboration and Faculty Work.* Greenwich, Conn.: Information Age Publishing, 2004.

Austin, A. E. "Preparing the Next Generation of Faculty: Graduate School as Socialization to the Academic Career." *Journal of Higher Education,* 2002, *73*(1), 94–122.

Bartlett, K. T. "Feminist Legal Methods." *Harvard Law Review,* 1990, *103,* 829–888.

Becher, T. *Academic Tribes and Territories: Intellectual Enquiry and the Cultures of Disciplines.* Bristol, Pa.: Society for Research into Higher Education and Open University Press, 1989.

Bennis, W. G. "Four Traits of Leadership." In J. N. Williamson (ed.), *Leader-Manager.* New York: Wiley, 1986.

Bensimon, E. M., and Neumann, A. *Redesigning Collegiate Leadership: Teams and Teamwork in Higher Education.* Baltimore, Md.: Johns Hopkins University Press, 1993.

Bolman, L. G., and Deal, T. E. *Reframing Organizations: Artistry, Choice and Leadership.* (2nd ed.) San Francisco: Jossey-Bass, 1997.

Doan, S. R. *The Collaborative Model: The Effective Model for the Increasing Interdependence of Organizations.* 1995. (ED 392 154)

Fairweather, J. S. *Faculty Work and Public Trust: Restoring the Value of Teaching and Public Service in American Academic Life.* Needham, Mass.: Allyn & Bacon, 1996.

Fear, F. A., and Sandmann, L. R. "Unpacking the Service Category: Reconceptualizing University Outreach for the 21st Century." *Continuing Higher Education Review,* 1997, *59*(3), 117–122.

Golde, C. M. "Beginning Graduate School: Explaining First-Year Doctoral Attrition." In M. S. Anderson (ed.), *The Experience of Being in Graduate School: An Exploration.* New Directions for Higher Education, no. 101. San Francisco: Jossey-Bass, 1998.

Kegan, R. *The Evolving Self: Problem and Process in Human Development.* Cambridge, Mass.: Harvard University Press, 1982.

Klein, J. T. *Interdisciplinarity: History, Theory, and Practice.* Detroit, Mich.: Wayne State University Press, 1990.

Kuhnert, K. W., and Lewis, P. "Transactional and Transformational Leadership: A Constructive/Developmental Analysis." In W. E. Rosenbach and R. L. Taylor (eds.), *Contemporary Issues in Leadership.* (2nd ed.) Boulder, Colo.: Westview Press, 1989.

Mezirow, J. *Transformative Dimensions of Adult Learning.* San Francisco: Jossey-Bass, 1991.

Morgan, G. *Images of Organizations.* (2nd ed.) Thousand Oaks, Calif.: Sage, 1999.

O'Looney, J. "Modeling Collaboration and Social Services Integration: A Single State's Experience with Developmental and Non-Developmental Models." *Administration in Social Work,* 1994, *18*(1), 61–86.

Salter, L., and Hearn, A. *Outside the Lines: Issues in Interdisciplinary Research.* Montreal and Kingston, Canada: McGill-Queen's University Press, 1996.

Sandmann, L., and M. Flynn. "A Model for Neighborhood Redevelopment Through University-Mediated Intervention: Evaluation Research Plan." East Lansing: Michigan State University, 1997.

Senge, P. M. *The Fifth Discipline: The Art and Practice of the Learning Organization.* New York: Doubleday, 1990.

Smyth, J. "A 'Pedagogical' and 'Educative' View of Leadership." In J. Smyth (ed.), *Critical Perspectives on Educational Leadership.* Bristol, Pa.: Falmer Press, 1989.

Tierney, W. G. "Organizational Culture in Higher Education: Defining the Essentials." In M. Peterson (ed.), *ASHE Reader in Organization and Governance in Higher Education.* New York: Ginn, 1991.

Tuckman, B. W. "Developmental Sequence in Small Groups." *Psychological Bulletin,* 1965, *6*(63), 384–389.

Vaill, P. B. "The Learning Challenges of Leadership." In *The Balance of Leadership and Followership Working Papers.* College Park, Md.: Academy of Leadership Press, 1997.

MARILYN J. AMEY is associate professor and program chair of the Higher, Adult, and Lifelong Education Programs at Michigan State University in East Lansing, Michigan.

DENNIS F. BROWN is executive director of the Association for the Study of Higher Education in East Lansing, Michigan.

4

A commitment to pursue problems from multiple angles, methods, and theoretical positions means that research teams require strategies to navigate the tensions and conflict that inevitably emerge, particularly when the intent is to find ways to integrate different disciplinary perspectives.

Insight from Multiple Disciplinary Angles: A Case Study of an Interdisciplinary Research Team

Elizabeth G. Creamer

With support from external funding that has been renewed a number of times, the six-person team featured in this case study has been conducting a longitudinal investigation of immigrant youth and families in an urban setting since the mid-1980s. Participants in the project began the project in kindergarten and are now approaching the end of high school. The team's leader is a prominent scholar who founded the project and has been with it since its inception. His qualities as an individual and as a leader play a strong role in shaping the social dynamics and practices of the team.

One of the reasons that I picked this case to present in this volume was that in addition to having multiple ways to triangulate the data, I had the additional advantage of access to a considerable number of publications that trace the evolution of the team's thinking. An internal document, the team's authorship guidelines, provided important context for understanding some of its practices.

I collected data for the case from multiple sources over the course of more than one year, including two interviews with the team leader, Steven (a pseudonym); observations and interaction with five members of the team while they were preparing for a conference presentation; and an hour-long interview with Paula, who joined the project in 1988 as a graduate student and is now a co–principal investigator (PI). I have written about different aspects of this team in another publication (Creamer, 2003).

NEW DIRECTIONS FOR TEACHING AND LEARNING, no. 102, Summer 2005 © Wiley Periodicals, Inc.

The comments I present here are, by and large, those of Steven. I have tried to achieve some level of poly-vocality, however, by capturing some of the subtle differences in viewpoints among team members. The case focuses on Steven's collaboration with Paula.

I offer the case study as a potential springboard for reflection about a number of topics relevant to members of interdisciplinary research teams, including strategies about how to productively pursue differences of opinion and build consensus.

Disciplinary Context

Steven began our first interview with some information that he thought was an essential context for understanding his collaborative relationship with Paula. Some of this reflects elements of his disciplinary socialization that he has chosen to reject. These decisions have had a long-term effect not only on the kinds of research questions Steven has chosen to pursue but also on how he has chosen to pursue them.

During his graduate program in clinical psychology, Steven grew disillusioned with his discipline and the approach to research of "endless testing" that led to "sword fighting" over minor details. Instead, he felt driven to "work on problems that really mattered" and to do something that would help him "figure out what might actually help kids and families." He decided that he was interested in "big problems." He defined these as issues that are not likely to go out of fashion, like reading achievement. The reason this is important to understand, he explained, is that "it leads to doing big projects. And you can't do big projects by yourself." This decision has led Steven to be a lifelong collaborator, and it has expanded the scope of the problem he studies. His collaborative relationship with Paula is only one of many he has sustained over the course of his career.

The decision to pursue big questions has also led Steven to a fairly well-articulated idea about how to make that possible. Relationships are central to his philosophy about effective teams and how to sustain them. "You cannot do research like that," he said, "unless you develop relationships and build teams and take seriously the whole notion of sustaining a major research operation over a long period of time."

Relational Dynamics and a Commitment to Mutuality

One of the cornerstones of Steven's leadership style is his belief that mentoring is the most important type of collaborative relationship. Steven described mentoring relationships as starting with a traditional hierarchical configuration—what he labels a master-apprentice model—but evolving to a coequal relationship. In his view, this kind of relationship becomes coequal after each person becomes a leader by demonstrating expertise in an area. For the relationship to be successful and sustained over a long period of time, he said:

You have to have the deliberate open strategy that you want this person to emerge as a coequal leader. This is an explicit part of my strategy. That everybody has to have their place in the spotlight. From the very beginning, you want even the greenest graduate student to start finding the area where they become the expert and a leader on the team.

In Steven's view, there is room for multiple leaders on a team. Credibility is secured by carving out an area of expertise. Every member of the team has the opportunity to develop an area of expertise and take the lead on a publication. In his view, this is key to joint productivity and team sustainability. I interpret it to reflect a commitment to reciprocity or mutuality.

Paula is not prepared to characterize her relationship with Steven as coequal. Laughing at the suggestion that their relationship was coequal, she said that while there is "a good deal of respect of ideas" and that they go into writing papers with equal status, there are differences in status that are apparent in other aspects of their work. Steven has access to resources, like priority in receiving secretarial support, that Paula does not feel she has. Paula credited the fact that Steven's working style is not authoritarian as the reason she has remained on the team so long.

The contribution of collaboration to Steven's vitality is evident in the enthusiasm he has for his work and his colleagues. It keeps him energized and returning to the campus lab at a time when many colleagues his age have an eye on retirement. Work "is more fun when you have a group of people you are working with who you love," he said.

A Commitment to Multiple Perspectives

There is another aspect of the model of an academic career that was part of Steven's socialization in graduate school that he has chosen to ignore: "You pick a particular area and a particular problem and you work on it and you just become incredibly focused on that and take a particular point of view." Instead, he believes that it is important to attack problems from many different directions. He is an enthusiastic advocate for the contribution of multiple viewpoints, methods, and theoretical interpretations to new insight.

In addition to what he derives from personal relationships, attacking problems from multiple perspectives is another juncture where enjoyment and learning occur for Steven. Anthropology fascinates him, as do powerful statistical techniques. He values the insight that can be gained by looking at a problem from multiple angles:

> Every time you look at the world from a little bit different angle, you learn something new. So, if you apply that to this kind of research . . . if you look at it from the point of view of the families, you get one take on it. If you look at it from the point of view of teachers, then you learn something else. I just am determined that it might be possible . . . to put all those things together and get some take on what is there. That is what I like to do.

Paula's learning is as boundary spanning as is Steven's. Her cultural view of family and schools has expanded the scope of the work of the team. At the same time, she has learned to become conversant with the powerful statistical tools that Steven and other members of the team employ.

Discursive Strategies Designed to Defuse Conflict

Steven acknowledges that an interdisciplinary approach often leads people to think they disagree when in fact they are looking at a problem or question from a different angle. When an exchange grows heated, Steven's discursive strategy is not to dismiss the differences or try to achieve consensus, but to try to push the exploration of how the multiple angles enrich the interpretation. Voicing an ability to juggle competing explanations, Steven said:

> Fortunately, most of the stuff we do, there hasn't been a single big idea, but there have been a few. They did reach some level of conflict . . . so what I have tried to do is to push it to make it easy to talk about. So you bring this up and start talking about it. The solution is to say, look, the data are what matter. So, collect your data. Let's publish your data, let's figure out the authorship, and as far as the project is concerned, you can publish contradictory data, but you've got to make sure that your data are reliable and valid. It must meet the highest standards. We are not going to argue about the idea. We will be in endless conflict about who got it first.

The example Steven picked to illustrate his point reflects a major challenge that some interdisciplinary collaborators face: how to reconcile differences in perspective that are grounded in fundamentally different ontological or epistemological assumptions. Although Steven minimized the depth of the disagreement, exchanges with other members of the team revealed that it has actually been a long-standing bone of contention between Paula and Chris, a senior member of the team who is recognized as the team's quantitative methodologist.

At Steven's prompting, Paula and Chris documented their different perspectives in publications appearing in different disciplinary journals. Chris served as lead author of one publication, Paula of another. In the publication in which Chris assumed the role of lead author, they combined qualitative and quantitative data to challenge a long-standing theoretical axiom in psychology. Paula appeared as third author on this article and wrote the section that presents the analysis of qualitative data. They reversed this pattern in a publication in which Paula presented a more cultural analysis of their findings.

The team members have different viewpoints about the resolution of this long-standing debate. In our second interview, Steven said that although he does not think it is that "big of a deal," he admitted, "When those two [Chris and Paula] start talking about it, they always seem to find some way to create a distinction." Later in the same interview he acknowledged the validity of both points of view.

To Paula's way of thinking, the two publications represent two entirely different points of view; she does not seem to share Steven's belief that both perspectives are right. When I asked her about the differences in viewpoint, she noted they had resurfaced in a recent exchange with Chris: "We were talking about qualitative and quantitative work. Talking about combining the two, Chris said, well, there really isn't that big of a difference. It isn't that big of a deal. Well, *yes* there is [said with emphasis]. It is a different way . . . so we kind of got off again into our camps."

Paula has difficulty reconciling the competing interpretations that emerged from analysis of the qualitative and quantitative data that neither Steven nor Chris shares. The differences she is reporting are fundamental epistemological differences about how knowledge is constructed. It happens that in this case, these also parallel differences in disciplinary grounding. As Paula and Chris have made abundantly clear after a decade of debate, these are fundamental differences in paradigmatic assumptions that are unlikely to be integrated in a collective perspective.

Discursive Strategies That Promote the Integration of Disciplinary Perspectives

Discursive practices help collaborators move beyond an individualistic or disciplinary stance to one that integrates knowledge from different domains. In addition to a culture that prizes the insight gained from looking at a problem from multiple perspectives, the multiple exchanges of an evolving manuscript and practices for handling authorship order and credit are discursive strategies that can promote the move from a disciplinary to an interdisciplinary perspective.

Exchanges That Advance Thinking. Steven described the writing of a manuscript as a process that generally takes months before everybody is satisfied. They approach the process not simply as one of routine editing and feedback, but one where ideas are significantly advanced by the insertion of questions ("probes") and comments in electronically transmitted documents. Differences in interpretation are often resolved during this process, as a probe might lead one of the authors to find additional data to document a point or reconsider a position when a step in the inferential process has been overlooked.

The electronic format creates a place for what Steven described as "distanced criticism." By this, I think he means that the distance afforded by the electronic format makes it easier to accept blunter feedback than might be the norm for face-to-face conversation. The specificity of the task of writing within the context of scrutiny provided by a collaborator comparably immersed in the research provides the type of informed feedback that can lead to learning and conceptual change. Physical proximity and dialogue are not as instrumental to the insight achieved by this team as I have found them to be among many of the long-term collaborators I have interviewed.

Authorship Guidelines. The authorship guidelines developed by this team and documented in an internally circulated publication is another discursive strategy the team deployed to defuse conflict. Part of the strategy is to minimize conflict by making authorship participation and credit an open process, subject to frequent discussion. Their strategy is to rely on "words on paper," that is, "sentences and paragraphs that survive into the final draft," to determine authorship credit and order. Relying on words on paper may provide a way to dodge contentious debates about who deserves primary credit for the intellectual content of a publication. Only people who actively contribute to the writing process and do so in a timely manner are listed as authors. No one is automatically entitled to credit as an author on a team-produced publication.

The role of the lead author prescribed by this team's authorship guidelines is not an unusual one. The first author is responsible for initiating the publication, doing the majority of writing, and carrying the manuscript through to publication. Second and third authors typically write sections of the manuscript and stay actively involved during the process of revisions.

The team's authorship guidelines explicitly acknowledge the potential for differences of opinion. Part of the stated purpose of the guidelines is to "establish an atmosphere in which there can be theoretical differences of opinion or varying interpretations of the data, but in which all are committed to the highest standards of qualitative and quantitative research." The guidelines are another discursive practice the team has used to normalize disputes that arise from different viewpoints.

The next part of this team's authorship guidelines may point to the juncture of their discursive practices that provided the leeway to sidestep a collective vision. The guidelines assign the lead author the responsibility for resolving "differences of opinion and varying interpretations of the data." In the example of the long-standing dispute between Paula and Chris, the practice of using a lead author and singular voice concealed the dispute, as did the tactic of airing different viewpoints in journals directed at different disciplinary audiences. Despite the value awarded to different viewpoints, this team has not built the integration of different viewpoints into their discursive practices.

Implications for Practice

This case study offers a number of insights about effective collaborative practices for practitioners launching or attempting to sustain a team effort and researchers investigating collaborative aspects of faculty life. These recognize that conflict and tension are central to understanding the interpretive process collaborators employ (Creamer, 2004).

Recommendations for Collaborators. This case is instructive in its revelations regarding discursive strategies that collaborators can use to defuse conflict in interdisciplinary projects. Perhaps the most obvious recommendation suggested by the case concerns the importance of crafting a culture that places a premium on the contribution of differences of opinion to new insight. A leader can attach positive connotations to conflict by casting it as routine, something that is to be expected, something that is enjoyable, or something that when pursued, has the potential to create significant new insight.

Written authorship guidelines and a team culture that treats authorship credit as something that is easy to talk about are practices that can defuse conflict and contribute to the sustainability of a team. Relying on "words on paper" to determine authorship rewards team members who remain engaged in the writing process in a timely way.

Insight About Research Practices. For qualitative researchers, this case study underscores the importance of triangulating data by supplementing interview data with observation and document analysis. In this case, the authorship guidelines provided critical context for interpreting a how a long-standing difference of opinion manifested itself in the way the team presented its findings to the public. Interaction with graduate students on the team introduced me to some issues that were not part of the way the leaders represented the team.

My experience in writing case studies has led me to underscore the importance of looking for differences, as well as similarities, among the viewpoints of participants. Interviews with a single member of a team, particularly when that person is a leader who is often an enthusiastic and articulate champion for the team, are unlikely to provide a multifaceted view of the workings of a research or teaching team. The team leader may present a vision of reality that is at odds with less powerful members of the team, as is evident in the differences between Steven and Paula's willingness to characterize their relationship as one of coequals.

Conclusions

I have cast this case within a sociocultural theoretical perspective that directs us to examine the impact of context on learning. In addition to exploring the individual qualities Steven demonstrated as a leader, I have considered how interpersonal relationships and social interaction are central to the processes of learning and constructing knowledge. A sociocultural perspective allows us to see that Steven's perspective about research is in some ways a departure from his disciplinary socialization and in some ways not. His productivity can be understood only when cast within the web of a number of collaborative relationships, of which the team is only one.

Steven and Paula are both enthusiastic about the advantages of an interdisciplinary perspective. Adapting an intentionally interdisciplinary approach has led Steven to a commitment to use multiple methodological methods, theories, and interpretations, without necessarily driving him to reconcile or integrate the contradictions this approach invites. In Paula's view, the interdisciplinary nature of the team has created multiple audiences for their work. She credits it with leading them to pursue a broader set of questions than was originally intended and with a greater willingness to experiment with different approaches. Part of what both Steven and Paula have learned is the social and discursive strategies to pursue research from the vantage point of multiple disciplines.

References

Creamer, E. G. "Exploring the Link Between Inquiry Paradigm and the Process of Collaboration." *Review of Higher Education*, 2003, *26*(4), 447–465.

Creamer, E. G. "Collaborators' Attitudes About Differences of Opinion." *Journal of Higher Education*, 2004, *75*(5), 556–571.

ELIZABETH G. CREAMER is associate professor of educational research and evaluation in the Department of Educational Research and Policy Studies at Virginia Tech in Blacksburg, Virginia.

5

Focused on an interdisciplinary graduate program in water resources management, this case study illustrates how theory-into-practice integration occurred in a field course and clarified students' expectations that faculty model interdisciplinary ways of knowing.

The Challenge of Integration in Interdisciplinary Education

Michele Minnis, Vera John-Steiner

There is a great distance between prescribing an interdisciplinary approach to resolve an educational problem and actually accomplishing such an approach. Although this chapter intends to illustrate that point, its larger purpose is to consider what achieving interdisciplinarity might entail.

Our case study concerns the professional education of decision makers in water-related fields, including managers of water utilities and other water systems, designers of water development projects, authors of water policy, and specialists in water and environmental law. Specifically, we focus on the nation's only professional master's degree in water resources, which is offered by the University of New Mexico (UNM) Water Resources Program. In its fourteen-year history, the program has produced a multifaceted water resources curriculum, enlisted as its faculty some of the university's most productive and respected professors, and attracted exceptionally sharp and dedicated graduate students. Even so, the program remains unsettled on basic questions about what it means in practical terms to call its enterprise interdisciplinary. Chiefly, these questions concern integration—what form it should take, whose job it is to make it happen, and how to determine the success of the effort. This chapter examines these questions in the light of a rich collection of student commentary on the program. These data were obtained over three years (2001–2003) from successive student cohorts

We gratefully acknowledge Mera Jane Triffler Wolf's expert contributions to this research as facilitator for the Focus Group on Interdisciplinary Education.

in the program's core interdisciplinary courses. We analyze this feedback from the students as a report of their expectations for an interdisciplinary experience and an indication of the issues confronting the faculty.

The Water Resources Program

A committee comprising UNM faculty members from eleven academic units as well as several campus institutes that sponsor water-related research and community outreach created the Water Resources Program (WRP) in 1991. The committee aimed to answer a recognized need for broadly educated water administrators, professionals capable of balancing diverse perspectives on water resources. Because effective water management depends on integrating knowledge across disciplines and applying it on the ground, the education of water resources professionals must be centrally concerned with the development of such abilities.

Curriculum. The result of the founders' efforts is a professional degree, the master of water resources (MWR), designed to provide students greater depth of knowledge in their primary disciplines while introducing them to a spectrum of disciplinary perspectives on water issues. The curriculum is both multidisciplinary and interdisciplinary. It is multidisciplinary in that all students take eighteen credit hours of WRP-approved graduate courses in the biological and earth sciences, civil engineering, water chemistry, watershed planning, resource economics, resource administration, and water and environmental law. Electives are chosen based on the student's career interests and choice of concentration, whether in a hydrosciences track or in a policy and management track.

Three interdisciplinary courses form the spine of the program, the core where its disparate parts intersect and, ideally, are integrated: Contemporary Issues, Models, and the capstone course, Field Project. The interdisciplinary courses are required of all students, must be taken in sequence, and are taught by faculty teams: four-member teams in the first two courses, a two-member team in the third. Enrollment in each course is limited to eighteen. Each of the three teaching teams has one member whose instruction focuses on communications skills.

Faculty. Almost all of the forty-two faculty members currently listed on the WRP Web site are full-time professors; thirty are male, and twelve are female. Twelve faculty members (29 percent) are from the Earth and Planetary Sciences Department; six (14 percent) are from civil engineering; and there are five each (12 percent) from the departments of Biology and Economics and the Division of Community and Regional Planning. A senior-level professor who teaches in all three core courses and heads the governing entity, a ten-member program committee, directs the program. Despite the concentration of WRP faculty in the earth sciences and civil engineering, membership on this committee is structured such that the social sciences, humanities, and professions are represented equally with the basic and life sciences.

Students. Of the more than sixty currently enrolled WRP students, the majority are returning students who have been out of college for at least five years and work full time or part time in water agencies or in private consulting firms concerned with water or the environment. They are evenly divided by gender. Although some have backgrounds in the humanities or the social sciences, most earned their undergraduate degrees in the basic sciences or engineering. Not surprisingly, considering that the program prerequisites are largely math and science courses, WRP students tend to be technically and quantitatively oriented. Few begin the program with extensive experience in sociocultural, economic, or policy analysis about water resources. On the whole, however, as indicated by their application letters, they seek the "integrated perspective on water in nature and society" promised in the program descriptions. This desire for a more holistic understanding of water systems than is provided by specialized academic programs fits with another common attribute of WRP students: an interest in making a practical difference in solving problems of water distribution or pollution.

The Interdisciplinary Core Courses

The WRP director and one of the authors serve on all three teaching teams for the core courses. They are the hydrologist and research psychologist, respectively, on the Contemporary Issues and Models teams and constitute the teaching team for Field Project.

The First Course: Contemporary Issues. Students ordinarily take this course during their first term in the program. It follows a lecture and discussion format and covers emerging and critical water-related problems around the world. Membership on the teaching team has been stable for the past four years. In addition to the two regular members, noted previously, there are a resource economist and a geographer who is also an attorney.

The communications emphasis is on critical reading and expository writing. Working as individuals or in small teams, the students write and present to the class an in-depth analysis of a particular water-related conflict. This analysis prepares students for interdisciplinary work because it requires them to define a problem in a real-world setting and address it by drawing on pertinent information from diverse sources, for example, historical, economic, social, cultural, hydrologic, legal, and political sources.

The Second Course: Models. In this course, students practice building rudimentary dynamic simulations of water systems and augmenting these basic models with economic variables. Here, the communications segment concerns design and use of data graphics. Course materials include texts utilizing STELLA modeling software and selected readings on presentation graphics. In addition to the hydrologist and research psychologist, the teaching team includes a civil engineer and an economist, both of them female. Thus, the team for Models, three women and one man, reverses the gender composition in Contemporary Issues, three men and one woman.

Models course work concerns a specific river reach and associated groundwater that constitute the water supply for a defined community or region. The locale changes from year to year. Assignments are made to teams of two, chosen by lot. The exception is the final assignment, for which there are teacher-designated four-member teams. Overall, the job of the teams is to clarify the water future of the selected region under several water use scenarios. After collecting data bearing on their inquiries, the teams represent the systems in stages. Using the course software, they build a model of annual surface water flow in the river reach. After presenting and comparing their models, the teams work as a whole to merge their models into one that combines the most desirable elements of each. Next, back in teams, the students model the groundwater that is tributary to the river reach; repeat the present, compare, and merge procedure with the groundwater model; and then couple the groundwater model to the surface water model. Finally, the teams introduce into the exercise regional demographic and socioeconomic data. In the final presentation, conducted as a briefing to residents of the selected region, the teams explain their integrated models and simulations of future water availability under hypothetical water use conditions.

The Final Course: Field Project. The final course in the interdisciplinary series and, for most students, in the program itself, is partly conducted out of the country. Field Project is a cooperative effort from start to finish. In groups of ten or fewer, students make a twelve-day trip to a village in Honduras and produce an extensive project report on their return. It contains a watershed model of the village, an analysis of the sustainability of local resource use practices in the village, and a sociological or educational product, such as a household survey or an environmental studies curriculum for the village children.

The destination in Honduras varies, but is always a subsistence farming community, located in the mountains along the country's northwest coast. As guests of the village (which has 250 to 700 residents), the students are lodged either in a community building or in their own tents and are provided three meals a day. In exchange, they work side by side with the villagers to build a gravity-flow system that will deliver potable water to individual households.

Building the water supply system means clearing a dam site in the rocky jungle above the village, making forms for a small concrete dam, leveling a tank site close to the village, digging a pit for the tank platform, and threading, cutting, and laying pipe between the dam and the tank. Participation in the course also includes getting acquainted with the local people and evaluating the design of the water delivery system. The latter includes collecting and analyzing water samples as well as discussing issues of agricultural practices; sanitation; supply, demand, and use of environmental resources; family, community, and institutional structures; and public education, public involvement, and community empowerment.

Summary of the Core Courses. In one way or another, and many times over, all three core courses oblige participants to integrate course content across disciplinary domains. By and large, however—even when integration is programmed into the syllabus—responsibility for conceptual integration defaults to the students as implicit assignments. Ordinarily members of the teaching team do not endeavor to detect and call out integration issues; neither do they deliberately enact or prescribe general approaches to integration. Accordingly, we were interested in knowing the extent to which students themselves perceived a need to integrate course material and, if so, in what kinds of circumstances and with what results.

Data Sources for the Case Study

We drew on three types of data: course evaluations over the past three years for all three core courses ($N = 117$), excerpts from students' Field Project journals ($N = 29$), and the products of a focus group for WRP students about interdisciplinary education ($N = 9$).

Course Evaluation Questionnaires. The interdisciplinary courses differ from standard university courses in that they are team-taught and there is a commitment to displaying and using several disciplinary frameworks. For these reasons, the WRP director arranged to have evaluation questionnaires tailored to each of the courses. Submitting a completed course evaluation form is required of everyone who is enrolled in a core course. Students answer the evaluation questionnaires anonymously and submit them to a program assistant, who compiles the results.

The format of the questionnaire is similar for all three courses and combines rating scale items and short-answer items that either elaborate on a rating scale response or offer recommendations. Questionnaire content has consistently focused on the main course components: discussion topics, readings, format, assignments, working in small groups or teams, communications instruction and exercises, general faculty involvement, and specific faculty contributions to the experience of the course. In every case, the evaluation form asks students to indicate their perceptions about the quality of their participation in the course and the relevance of the course to their career plans.

Field Project Student Journal. In the field course, students are required to keep a journal in which they record impressions and experiences. They are offered several suggestions for approaches they might take in writing their journal, including to (1) summarize and comment on data collection and other observations at the work sites; (2) consider and compare with their own culture specific practices they observed in the host community; (3) sketch pictures of persons, things, or events they wish to remember; (4) write of home and things familiar; and (5) use later entries to comment on earlier ones.

Although the journals are not graded (and not even read by the teachers), students are required to represent them in an appendix to the final report they prepare for the Field Project. For this section of the report, course participants select their own submissions, either quoting from their journals or summarizing several entries. These excerpts have averaged one to two pages in length.

Focus Group on Interdisciplinary Education. At the end of the fall 2003 term, after classes had ended and grades had been posted, we organized a lunch and focus group. An invitation to participate was mailed to all WRP students who had completed at least one of the core courses. The invitation included details about time and place, as well as a brief explanation about who had been invited and announcements that participation was voluntary, that the focus group was part of our study on interdisciplinary education, and that the group discussion would be facilitated by a colleague who was experienced in group facilitation but unknown to the WRP students.

At the focus group session and as a warm-up for the group discussion, the facilitator asked each participant to read and sign a consent form and, anonymously, fill out a worksheet. The consent form explained that although the sponsors of the focus group were concerned mainly with interdisciplinary teaching teams, they were also interested in how students experienced courses taught by such teams.

The worksheets asked questions about which WRP interdisciplinary courses the respondents had completed and whether they had taken interdisciplinary courses prior to entry in the program. In addition, the worksheets allowed a half-page for handwritten answers to each of the following questions:

"Think about and jot down differences you've noticed between courses taught by multidisciplinary teams and courses taught by a single instructor."

"In practical terms, what have those differences meant for you, as a student in those courses?"

"Do you notice any personal changes that you would attribute to taking an interdisciplinary, team-taught course(s)?"

"Consider the costs and benefits that you associate with team-taught courses. Do they balance out?"

Once the participants had finished the paperwork, the facilitator began the discussion and moderated an exchange that continued for slightly over two hours.

Analysis and Results

Our analysis generally followed the methodology of grounded theory (Glaser and Strauss, 1973; Dick, 2002; Charmaz, 2004). Briefly, that is, we treated the data corpus as if it were a collection of musical notes from which, through systematic sorting and creative listening, meaningful themes might be derived.

The Two Classroom-Based Courses. Because the two classroom-based courses, Contemporary Issues and Models, were similar in many ways and so different in form from Field Project, we postponed summarizing the Field Project course evaluations until we had completed analysis of the Contemporary Issues and Models data. We began with the typed compilations of responses to the course evaluation questionnaires. These summaries presented responses to rating scale items as frequency distributions on a five-point scale that ranged from 1 (*strongly disagree*) to 5 (*strongly agree*). Answers to short-answer items and impromptu comments were reported verbatim for all respondents.

Evaluations. The Contemporary Issues evaluations contained the responses of fifty-one students to questionnaires containing twenty to twenty-two items. None of these items directly addressed our focal interest: how students recognize and deal with issues of conceptual integration across disciplinary frameworks. Therefore, while considering all the evaluation data, we concentrated on rating scale and short-answer responses to the six items concerning course components that seemed likely to prompt remarks about content integration: course format, course project, student teams, professors' support, self-evaluation of performance, and course success. Because the Contemporary Issues ratings showed a consistent pattern from year to year, we collapsed data across years in summarizing them. These summaries indicate high student satisfaction with Contemporary Issues. For each of the six items rated, the preponderance of responses, 70 percent, lay in the top two affirmative rating positions (a 4 or a 5).

The course evaluation data for Models contained the responses of thirty-four students to a questionnaire of seventeen to twenty-five items. The Models and Contemporary Issues questionnaires differed in detail. Thus, the six questionnaire items, or course components, that we examined closely also differed. For Models, the components were career relevance of the course, course organization, assignments, professors' feedback, lectures and discussions, and readings and handouts. The ratings for Models were less robustly positive than were those for Contemporary Issues; only 43 percent of the responses lay in the two highest positions (a 4 or a 5). Moreover, responses to the question about professors' feedback on assignments were distributed such that one-third lay in the low end, one-third in the middle, and one-third in the high end. Overall, however, the ratings were more affirmative than not: 70 percent of the Models ratings lay in the three highest positions on the scale (a 3, 4, or 5).

Students' Comments. As we delved into the questionnaire data, the picture of high regard for Contemporary Issues and general satisfaction with Models became more complex and, in some respects, contradictory. This more shaded rendering was provided by the students' comments. On first examining the comments, we considered each only in the light of the specific questionnaire item that had prompted it. After becoming familiar with the range and content of the comments, however, we began to group them according to the direction of the recommendation (for example, "keep this practice," "discard that one"). Using these new categories, we observed but a few suggestions that a course component or activity be totally eliminated. Much more common were recommendations that, while implying "Retain x," stated, "Do x much better" (or earlier in the semester, or less often, or, in this context, rather than that, or with this kind of preparation and followup). Typically, qualifying remarks of this sort might indicate nothing more than an appeal to "tidy up the course." Some of these messages appeared so frequently and in such an insistent tone, however, that they called for close attention. Accordingly, we collected and tabulated all recommendations for future offerings of Contemporary Issues and Models.

Student recommendations for both Contemporary Issues and Models show appreciation of the teachers' expertise, the value of group work, and the merits of the research and writing assignments. More than one-third of the Contemporary Issues recommendations (105 of 286, or 37 percent) were to retain a course component; for Models, the comparable data represented just under one-fifth of the total (30 of 164 responses, or 18 percent).

Less favorable comments were in evidence as well. In view of our interest in content integration, the most earnest and telling recommendations concerned the teachers' performance not as scholars or as individuals but as a team. The gist of these, expressed as a complaint, was that the novelty, complexity, and difficulty of these courses demanded much greater involvement by the faculty than was provided. Relevant comments called for greater coordination among the teachers about assignments and expectations of students, more detailed and timely feedback on student work, and, particularly, better modeling of interdisciplinary interaction.

In the area that might be called "support from the teaching team," the message conveyed by the comments of many Models students was that they sometimes felt overwhelmed, frustrated, or angered by the assignments and wanted far more teacher involvement in their work on the assignments than was forthcoming.

Recapping the evaluations of Contemporary Issues and Models, we found that when central course components were rated separately on Likert-type scales, the picture was one of respectable, if not strong, student support. At the same time, the more nuanced comment data revealed that while the students accepted that an interdisciplinary program is challenging in many ways, they expected more straightforward direction from the faculty and more modeling of interdisciplinarity in the faculty's own ways of planning and interacting. These recommendations were also voiced, even amplified, in the focus group.

Focus Group Data. A focus group for WRP students was conducted between the fall and spring semesters, just after the end of a Contemporary Issues course. Of the nine students attending, five had taken all three core courses; the other four had taken only the first, Contemporary Issues. All were in academic good standing, and one was a recent graduate. In that setting, an open forum of peers and with a facilitator primed to listen carefully, it appeared that the students were emboldened to express criticism more sharply. The facilitator's report described the general tone of a discussion comparing courses taught by individual instructors and multidisciplinary teams as "mixed . . . but more negative than positive." Not surprisingly, considering that it was the single course all participants had in common, the students drew examples from the team for Contemporary Issues. For example, according to the facilitator,

> Although the multiple perspectives of the instruction were viewed universally by the respondents as a "good thing" in the abstract, again and again comments were made questioning the "delivery system," and expressions of frustration dominated the conversation. Just one of the participants expressed a high degree of comfort with the instructors' "competing claims, styles, expectations, and tones."

The question of the relative merits of having a solo instructor versus a multidisciplinary team also was posed on the focus group worksheets and the course evaluation questionnaires for Contemporary Issues 2003. Summary of those two sources on that issue yielded the following information. The pros for solo instruction and the cons for team instruction were reciprocals of one another. Whereas students saw having one teacher as advantageous in terms of predictability (coming to understand instructor's style, instructions, expectations, and standards) and reliability (one person responsible for the development and success of the course), having multiple teachers was seen as disadvantageous for opposite reasons (as a team, teachers are disorganized, disagree on expectations of students, vary in teaching styles, are unrealistic about how much can be learned in one semester, sacrifice depth for breadth, and fail to build on each other's work or hold each other accountable for contributing equally to the development and success of the course). Yet team teaching was said to offer its own positive attributes—for example, variety in teaching styles, critique of one's work from more than one source, multiple views from multiple angles, broader knowledge base, and "unstructured/unplanned interplay between professors, whether agreeing or not, can lead to lots of learning and more critical thinking skills."

According to the facilitator, the focus group participants were in consensus about the uncertainties created by the team-teaching approach:

There were many concerns surrounding the uncertainty of their grades, especially given the instructors' different expectations, how vulnerable [the students] were in this situation, and how dependent they were upon the instructors for their "future." Most felt that they could not speak freely, comment in class, or attempt to redirect the class discussions to something more productive for this reason.

Another telling comment, agreed to by all, was that their class assignments were many, long, and difficult. Although they felt that these had real value and that virtually all of them had relevance, genuine feelings of anger "erupted" in our discussion as they remembered the many times in class when it became clear to them that there would be little or no follow-up. There were few interactions with the instructors regarding their substantial efforts or their many questions about these assignments.

Field Project. Having seen the evaluations of the first two core courses, we next turned to those for Field Project. Here we were struck by the difference in tone and a virtual chorus of praise. The following excerpts from the course evaluations and student journals address the fieldwork proper, general impressions of the course, and the appropriateness of the course as the program capstone:

> I think the best thing I learned was just an appreciation for the difficulties of putting in a water system. There are problems beyond the simple design of the project that must be considered, and ones you can never plan for.

> Don't think that it is an overstatement to say that our trip to Honduras was a life-changing event. It was for me and I think most in our group felt the same way as I do. There is just nothing negative that I can say.

> This class brought all the previous courses together in a real world experience.

Implicit throughout these data is the message that Field Project provided students interdisciplinary integration-in-action. But the students' remarks suggested that they experienced the course as more than bringing together and applying different fields of knowledge. It appears that the field experience also generated a degree of commitment and had an emotional impact that overcame any sense of disconnection between self and community. Several students expressed elation and pride that, individually and collectively, they had been up to the task. Reported benefits included professional and personal growth; greater understanding of daily life in the Third World, especially respect for people raised differently—and admiration for the hard work and endurance witnessed; the importance of building relationships with the people one serves or works with; the unique privilege of the opportunity to participate; and gratitude for the feeling of being truly useful.

Summary. Although the course evaluation questionnaires did not include course-to-course comparisons, the data cluster in ways that suggest a comparative evaluation. On this point, we observed consistencies of two types: (1) in failings noted for the first two courses but not for the third and (2) in successes attributed to the third but not to the first two. The teaching teams for Contemporary Issues and for Models were frequently criticized as being poorly coordinated among themselves, presenting disparate, if not contradictory, messages about assignment definitions and performance expectations, and ignoring student desires for feedback. Moreover, the teachers were often described as deeply engaged in their respective disciplinary subjects but disengaged from the course as a whole. In short, the teaching teams were said to have left a vacuum, where they might have built bridges, for the students' benefit, across the conceptual divides among them.

The Field Project data contained no critiques on these points. What they do contain are affirmative comments of a type rarely found in evaluations of the two other courses. Students of the field course described it as immediately meaningful, emotionally and professionally, in that it required them to gather and apply, to evidently satisfying effect, various kinds of knowledge they had gained previously. In addition, they consistently commended the teachers for working well as a team, preparing them for the fieldwork, working with them in the field, and supporting them throughout the course. In comparison with the two other core courses, Field Project gave students the greater, more satisfying sense of integration.

Conclusions

Our study has revealed that students value the WRP highly. It has also shown that on entering the program, the students knew and accepted that the interdisciplinary courses would present unusual challenges. Their genuinely fervent support was mixed, however, with a bit of loyal opposition. Their comments indicated widely shared expectations that the teaching teams would provide consistent direction and feedback, hands-on support, and, through classroom interactions, working models of interdisciplinary communication. For most students, apparently, these hopes were not entirely fulfilled in the Contemporary Issues and Models courses but largely realized in Field Project.

Although there are many ways to view and interpret the course evaluation data, we focused on the issues mentioned in the preceding paragraph. We grouped them under the heading "integration," assuming that this term named the students' general concern, as well as the operational path to interdisciplinarity. That is, we saw integration as a matter of creating a new center and dynamic among separate disciplines. Had we dealt only with the evaluations of Contemporary Issues and Models, we might have concluded, as the students did, that integrating course material was mainly the teachers' responsibility and, in this case, not a fully successful one. But student responses to Field Project led us to think more deeply.

In Field Project, the problem of integrating course content vanished as an issue. The problem resolved itself as the students departed the classroom, where knowing is disaggregated and abstracted, and were reintroduced, as a group and with a task assignment, into the world of immediate sense experience—what William James called the "big blooming buzzing confusion" (James, 1979, p. 32). Certainly the students' previous class work, as well as their familiarity and teamwork with each other, prepared them to act effectively and learn from the village water project in the manner of Schön's "reflective practitioners" (1983). The students' accounts of this work as meaningful and whole in its impact are unsurprising. This effect may have come more from removal of academic inhibitors to integration as from any affirmative interventions by the teachers.

Nonetheless, in providing a positive instance of integration, Field Project revealed how limiting our assumptions had been about what integration might mean in an interdisciplinary context. We had been thinking of integration narrowly, as a conceptual accomplishment, the construction of merged or expanded cognitive frameworks. Field Project gave us something else—theory-into-practice integration—and thereby opened the window on myriad possible meanings, moments, levels, and loci of interdisciplinary integration. That recognition brought others—for example, that the educator's role in preparing students to make the most of integrating possibilities is contingent on circumstances, on who, what, when, why, and how. To us, integration began to seem less in the nature of a once-and-finished thing and more in the nature of an attitude of openness and expectancy.

Was integration-in-action a necessary consequence of Field Project? Could it be expected to occur in any experiential course in an interdisciplinary context? Ours is not the kind of controlled experiment that would allow confident answers to either question, and answers might depend on the type and degree of integration one had in mind. In the case of the field course, the shared intensity and other unusual features of the experience would have made it memorable for any group of students at any point in a graduate program. But we think it more likely that the integrative experience of Field Project was a cumulative effect and that the field experience would have been much less professionally meaningful to the students without the technical and conceptual underpinning provided by Contemporary Issues and by Models. No doubt the indelible impact of the field course resulted from the interaction of many variables: the students' common history with each other and the field course teachers in the two prior courses, the students' maturation in their chosen concentration areas, and the camaraderie and joint commitment engendered by the opportunity to build something that measurably improved the daily existence of several hundred people. Additional probable contributions to the richness of the students' experience were the villagers' organization of the project, related materials, and the work plan, as well as their preparation for and welcoming of the students' visit and assistance.

In effect, the students themselves were integrated into a preindustrial village where holistic learning and practice is a necessary part of daily life and mutual dependence is an inescapable norm: all of one's time is absorbed by the tasks of obtaining water, growing and preparing food, and looking after livestock and small children. There is no opting out. The students were assigned to make the most of the circumstances, consider them reflectively in their journals, and cooperatively tell the relevant hydrologic story in the language of a technical model. It is not surprising that they regarded the course as a watershed experience.

The students' response to the field course setting brings to mind Rogoff's concepts of "guided participation" (1990) and "transformation of participation" (1998), which she advanced in her research on early childhood development. Rogoff assumes that new skills, as well as new perspectives and ways of thinking, become one's own not through solitary work but through collaborative processes. Clarifying these processes, Rogoff borrows from Vygotsky (Vygotsky and others, 1978) the term *zone of proximal development* (ZPD), to refer to the space where the process occurs. In any learning context, from the point of view of the learner, the ZPD is the space lying just beyond one's current level of performance or understanding, a gap one can traverse with the supportive guidance of more adept practitioners. Guided participation, then, is the mutually creative induction that communities afford their newest (or youngest) members through all sorts of ZPDs. Rogoff emphasizes that learners and guides are equally active: learners become skilled participants in the society through "routine, and often tacit, guided participation in ongoing cultural activities as they observe and participate with others in culturally organized practices" (1990, p. 16). As a learner proceeds, bringing to bear on her efforts feedback from the guidance and knowledge gained previously in other contexts, her participation is transformed, becoming both more skilled and uniquely hers. At the same time, the guides are also transformed in their knowing and roles. Critical to Rogoff's conception of guided participation is the reliance on intersubjectivity, that is, the mutual recognition by participants in a shared activity of cognitive, social, and emotional exchanges among them.

What Rogoff ascribes to the development of young children may apply as well to the water students' participation in the villages. At the fieldwork sites and in all their dealings with the host community and its unfamiliar culture, the students were guided by their own previous experience outside of and before the program and during the program with fellow students. They also depended on the experience of the faculty and the villagers, and at the same time, they guided each other.

Echoes of this analysis can be heard in Fuller and Unwin's remark, "The key to the development of learners is seen to be the quality of interactions which accompany the undertaking of authentic tasks" (1998, p. 164). Developing this idea, these authors summarize Finnish activity theorist Yrjo Engeström's writing on instruction and learning in working life (Engeström, 1994) in the following list of "ingredients of effective learning," all of which were present in Field Project:

- Access to theoretical and experiential knowledge
- The opportunity to engage in authentic tasks and interactions with others
- The chance to develop critical and intellectual capacities through the application of concepts and theories in practice
- The opportunity to have [one's] thinking and understanding enhanced through the guidance and teaching of others [Engeström, 1994, p. 48, cited in Fuller and Unwin, 1998, p. 161].

We have no specific evidence indicating that one of these ingredients was more important than another in the overall effect on the students. Many of the students' concurrent and retrospective remarks suggest that they considered the field experience to be physically, intellectually, and emotionally challenging; that they relied heavily on each other; and that the sense of integrated understanding they reported was more than bringing together different fields of knowledge and integrating them in action. It was also a matter of discovering the connection between self-knowledge, career knowledge, and the daunting challenges of water management in the global setting where this knowledge might be applied.

Educators may ask how our findings concerning integrated learning speak to their practice. They may wonder whether student distress in wrestling with integration in team-taught courses like Contemporary Issues and Models is unavoidable. Researchers and scholars concerned with interdisciplinarity (for example, Klein, 1996; Newell, 2001; Rhoten, 2003) may inquire how this investigation contributes to the developing field of integrative studies. The following section begins to address those questions.

Implications of Findings for Faculty

The current generation of senior-level faculty members is the first to be called on in numbers to move into the interdisciplinary sphere. In effect, then, many professors are in a ZPD with respect to interdisciplinary thought and instruction. To whom can they look for guidance? Who are the models?

More the exception than the rule, we would venture, is the accomplished professor who easily adopts the role of interdisciplinarian. What makes that step difficult? Partly, it is that in an interdisciplinary arena, disciplinary competence can be a two-edged sword. For example, interdisciplinary teaching obliges professors, who have been socialized to prize individual achievement, to add to their repertoires collaborative working methods—even where the prevailing reward structure runs counter to that. There are other self-references that may be challenged by entering the interdisciplinary domain—one's status as an expert, for example. Where being recognized for expertise is central to one's identity, participation in interdisciplinary work can pose an emotional risk comparable to cross-cultural travel. In academic communities, one's disciplinary training is one's home, the arena in which assumptions, language conventions, conceptual frameworks, evaluation standards, methods of inquiry, and even long-running disputes are second nature, familial. To depart that safe zone and experience oneself a novice in another disciplinary space may feel threatening. Asking basic questions, misunderstanding specialized terminology, being observed in the process of learning, even voicing what are accepted generalizations in one's own field— all of these actions may take on a different hue outside home territory. All the more is such exposure likely to feel risky when it occurs in front of students and differently trained peers—people to whom one looks for assurance of one's professorial competence.

If interdisciplinary teaching makes what might be termed countercultural demands on academics, how might they be assisted across the ZPD from discipline-centered solo instruction to interdisciplinary-centered team teaching? Rhoten's work on interdisciplinary collaboration in research settings may offer a lead. Rhoten (2003) examined patterns of interactions at several of the country's most prestigious interdisciplinary research centers. Key roles she identified among participants in these centers were those of "hubs" and "bridges" (p. 6). Hubs are those individuals who are "most connected to all other researchers in the center." While *hub* may be an uncommon term in the literature of collaboration, it is easy to appreciate that in a large institutional structure, hub roles might be assumed by several individuals, including, for example, both program directors and center directors. Bridge roles have been cited as critical functions in our own (John-Steiner, Weber, and Minnis, 1998) and other writings (Chubin, Porter, Rossini, and Connolly, 1986) on collaboration. Bridges are "researchers who have the most cross-disciplinary connections to other researchers in the center" (Rhoten, 2003, p. 6). Rhoten's study also classified interactions by function: either primarily information exchange or primarily knowledge creating in their effects. She treats the latter as more significant from the point of view of interdisciplinary productivity. Her summary about the distributions of roles and interactions may be somewhat unexpected:

> We found that with the exception of some overlap by some of the center directors, those who occupy the "hub" positions in a network are not the same individuals who serve as the interdisciplinary "bridges" in a network. Whereas the former are often content experts in their respective fields (regardless of rank), the latter are most often graduate students and/or frequently methodologists or technicians [p. 6].

Rhoten attributes the centrality of the graduate students as bridges in the research centers to their motivations: "The graduate students in our sample were often the most enthusiastic about the need for, and were engaged in the scholarly practices of, interdisciplinary research" (p. 5). The graduate students, in the initiation phases of acquiring professional identity, may well have had less at stake than full professors in appearing naive and may have perceived more to be gained in exploring other disciplinary frameworks. Rhoten's finding suggests that the connector function, especially the bridge role, is critical to interdisciplinary endeavors and is enacted by persons who prize the success of the work as interdisciplinary in nature.

We see the following implication of this finding for interdisciplinary teams. Interdisciplinary teaching requires a differentiated team effort. Planning the course syllabus is not enough. The functions of cross-disciplinary communication and integration must also be part of the plan. Rhoten's work (2003) and our own (John-Steiner, Weber, and Minnis, 1998) suggest that teaching-team planning, while giving time and space to content knowledge, must ensure that someone in the group—ideally a member who exhibits the intellectual curiosity and enthusiasm characteristic of Rhoten's bridges—consciously and seriously undertakes the bridge role. Among other things, adopting such a role would entail naming integration as a learning goal to be addressed in its own right. Related activities might include:

Facilitating cross-disciplinary communication within the multidisciplinary teaching team, either in team meetings or during class periods

Preparing the course syllabus and for individual class sessions with an eye to detecting, as points of departure for discussion, interdisciplinary disconnects in assumptions, priorities, scales, and units of analysis

Encouraging students and teachers to recognize and report, for benefit of discussion, occasions when they asked themselves, "How would an ecologist [a water lawyer, a geographer, a cultural historian] view this situation?"

Reviewing assigned readings and drafts of students' papers with the intention of identifying places where introduction of an alternative disciplinary frame might enrich the scholarship

Assigning students to create metaphors for both disciplinary and interdisciplinary perspectives on the course subject or a complex of issues being considered in the course.

No doubt, as some of these approaches are tried, others will suggest themselves. The idea is to bring the topic of integration to the light rather than leave it latent.

At the beginning of the chapter, we used the term *integration* without explanation or reference, thereby avoiding its multiplicity. The process of the case study has shown us that interdisciplinary integration can be viewed from the point of view of content integration or integration of theory and practice. In some ways, both kinds of integration, and at several levels, are involved in the entire water resources program. Our study, focusing strictly on the core courses, has illustrated theory-into-practice integration in the field course, documented student demand for greater cross-content integration in the two interdisciplinary classroom courses, and clarified the indispensability of bridge persons, or bridging functions, in interdisciplinary teaching teams.

We have a final caution, a caveat about patience: Building a new mode of thinking and teaching is a complex process and, for that reason, a long one. Cycles of construction, evaluation, revision, and reconstruction are essential developmental struggles in such a process.

References

Charmaz, K. "Grounded Theory." In D. N. Hesse-Biber and P. Leave (eds.), *Approaches to Qualitative Research: A Reader on Theory and Practice.* New York: Oxford University Press, 2004.

Chubin, D. E., Porter, A. L., Rossini, P. F., and Connolly, C. (eds.). *Interdisciplinary Analysis and Research: Theory and Practice of Problem-Focused Research and Development.* Mount Airy, Md.: Lomond, 1986.

Dick, R. "Grounded Theory: A Thumbnail Sketch." 2002. http://www.scu.edu.au/schools/gcm/ar/arp/grounded.html.

Engeström, Y. *Training for Change: New Approach to Instruction and Learning in Working Life.* Geneva: International Labour Office, 1994.

Fuller, A., and Unwin, L. "Reconceptualising Apprenticeship: Exploring the Relationship Between Work and Learning." *Journal of Vocational Education and Training,* 1998, 50(2), 153–173.

Glaser, B. G., and Strauss, A. L. *The Discovery of Grounded Theory: Strategies for Qualitative Research.* Chicago: Aldine, 1973.

James, W. *Some Problems of Philosophy.* Cambridge, Mass.: Harvard University Press, 1979. (Originally published 1911.)

John-Steiner, V., Weber, R. J., and Minnis, M. "The Challenge of Studying Collaboration." *American Educational Research Journal,* 1998, 35(4), 773–783.

Klein, J. T. *Crossing Boundaries: Knowledge, Disciplinarities, and Interdisciplinarities.* Charlottesville: University Press of Virginia, 1996.

Newell, W. H. "A Theory of Interdisciplinary Studies." *Issues in Integrative Studies,* 2001, 19, 1–25.

Rhoten, D. *A Multi-Method Analysis of the Social and Technical Conditions for Interdisciplinary Collaboration.* San Francisco: Hybrid Vigor Institute, 2003.

Rogoff, B. *Apprenticeship in Thinking: Cognitive Development in Social Context.* New York: Oxford University Press, 1990.

Rogoff, B. "Cognition as a Collaborative Process." In W. Damon (series ed.), D. Kuhn, and R. S. Siegler (eds.), *Handbook of Child Psychology,* Vol. 2: *Cognition, Perception, and Language.* New York: Wiley, 1998.

Schön, D. A. *The Reflective Practitioner: How Professionals Think in Action.* New York: Basic Books, 1983.

Vygotsky, L. S., and others. *Mind in Society: The Development of Higher Psychological Processes.* Cambridge, Mass.: Harvard University Press, 1978.

MICHELE MINNIS *is adjunct professor of water resources at the University of New Mexico.*

VERA JOHN-STEINER *is Presidential Professor of Linguistics and Education at the University of New Mexico.*

6

What do we learn about interdisciplinary collaboration and faculty learning from the three cases presented in Chapters Three to Five? What ideas will higher education researchers, faculty development practitioners, academic leaders, and professors want to consider?

Observations: Taking Seriously the Topic of Learning in Studies of Faculty Work and Careers

Anna Neumann

My role in this volume is to bring a learning perspective, anchored in research on educational practice, to bear on the three cases presented in Chapters Three to Five. I thereby review the cases in the light of the educational conundrum of what it means to know and what it takes to change what and how we know. In particular, I focus on the knowing, and changes in knowing, of professors whose primary practice is the shaping of what and how others know. They pursue this practice through diverse forms of academic work: teaching, research, outreach, service, and other academic activities.

Although in higher education we typically discuss knowing and learning as student experiences, they apply as well to professors' work experiences (Lattuca, 2001, 2002; Neumann, 2000; Kohn, 1990). Yet rarely do we talk in depth about what it means for professors to learn (Menges and Austin, 2001). This chapter adds to the volume's conversation about interdisciplinarity and collaboration by expanding on a key tenet: that sociocultural views speak to what it means, and what it takes, to know and to learn. However, because sociocultural theory arose in the context of prior theories about human learning and development, we must recognize that its content is deeply informed by them (Greeno, Collins, and Resnick, 1996). We must also acknowledge that research in the field of education broadly, and higher education specifically, typically relies on more than a single guiding theory, perspective, or discipline. Rather, educational phenomena lend themselves to interdisciplinary scrutiny. We might go so far as to assert

NEW DIRECTIONS FOR TEACHING AND LEARNING, no. 102, Summer 2005   © Wiley Periodicals, Inc.

that our understanding of the complexity and internal variation of educational activities, experiences, and artifacts is likely to be enhanced by the epistemological diversity (Pallas, 2001) that an interdisciplinary research team is likely to offer. To improve educational practices, we need not engage in contests that would pit one theory or perspective against another. Rather, we must choose and blend judiciously, given the variety available to us, shaping theory selectively for use in particular situations.

Given the field of education's primary devotion to the understanding of educational phenomena, and concomitant strivings for epistemological diversity and flexibility to support its pursuit, I strive in this chapter for a practice-anchored educational view of interdisciplinary collaboration in faculty work (for related perspectives, see Cohen, McLaughlin, and Talbert, 1993; Lampert, 2001; Prawat and Peterson, 1999; Putnam and Borko, 2000). In doing so, I remain true to the view of learning afforded by the sociocultural lens, as introduced in Chapter Two. However, I also draw out the sociocultural view, analyzing and reshaping it relative to the contours of diverse educational practices, some represented in the prior cases and others that I provide for illustration. In doing so, I seek to underline how images of professorial practice (whether research, teaching, outreach, or service) that take these academic practitioners' learning seriously may offer improved understandings of their work, as well as how, with time and thought, their work can change.

To address this aim of framing professors' interdisciplinary collaboration in ways that are true to education as itself an interdisciplinary endeavor, I frame my observations on the three preceding cases as an initial response to these questions: Given the images of interdisciplinary collaboration provided in these chapters, what can we learn about learning itself as potentially a core strand of faculty work? What might a learning perspective anchored in the situatedness that is central to sociocultural theory help us to understand about faculty work and lives? What images of faculty development, as a life span process, might a learning perspective yield? These are truly large questions that we have just begun to plumb. My goal, however, is limited: to distill from the preceding cases, and to some extent from my own studies of professors' learning and development, a few ideas worthy of consideration by others. Five ideas emerge as central (though clearly not as inclusive of all that can be said about faculty learning):

Faculty work implies faculty learning.
Talk and thought about learning is vague and insubstantial without taking into account what is being learned.
Professors' work is likely to involve learning defined as the creation, elaboration, refinement, or reconstruction of various practices—epistemic and discursive, social and cultural—and thus that what professors learn may in fact be such practices.

To understand what professors are learning requires attention to the contexts of their learning, since at times the learning context converts into
the learning content.

To facilitate collaboration by faculty representing diverse disciplines, perspectives, interests, and points of view, it may be helpful to position the
object of collaboration as a well-defined, authentic problem, itself
supradisciplinary (that is, exceeding any one discipline's purview) though
receptive to team members' concerted interdisciplinary (between disciplines) attention and action.

In the remainder of this chapter, I discuss these claims and their implications for improved understandings of professors' work—in research, outreach, and teaching—as presented in the case studies of professors'
interdisciplinary collaboration.

Claims: Learning from the Cases

A review of each case and comparative analysis of the three leads to the following claims about the nature of faculty learning and how we might think
about it.

Claim 1: Faculty Work as Faculty Knowing and Learning. I begin
with the claim that faculty work may be viewed in good part as acts of cognition, of knowing, for to do the work involves getting to know the work.
Certainly how a professor knows her or his work may change. The professor may come to see and think about it differently or in altogether new
ways. Such learning may be intentional, for example, as a person struggles
for new perspective; or it may be incidental, for example, as a person learns,
through conversations with others, about new ways to think about work.
Thus, from a cognitive perspective, professors' work implies the possibility
of their learning about research, teaching, outreach, or service as they
engage in these activities, prepare to do so, or look back on them reflectively
upon their completion (Lin and Schwartz, 2003; Schön, 1983, 1987). This
view begs for a definition of learning, and thus, I offer the following:
Learning, as changed cognition, involves the personal and shared construction of knowledge; it involves coming to know something familiar in
different ways, or to know something altogether new, from within one's self
and often with others. To learn is personal because it involves unique experiences of mind, limited in their transferability to others (Krieger, 1991;
Neumann, 1998). Yet this work of the mind is also deeply interactive in that
it draws on and produces cognitive connection among individuals who
come to know related things (Baltes and Staudinger, 1996; Wertsch, Del
Rio, and Alvarez, 1995), at times in unusual, even startlingly creative new
ways (see John-Steiner, 2000). In its connection to knowing, we may say
also that learning always involves knowledge—its making or remaking,

elaborating or refining. As we shall soon see, in speaking of learning or inquiring into its processes and effects, it is helpful to specify what knowledge is at issue, since experiences of knowing and learning are fully dependent on what is known and learned. We learn only because we have or create something to learn, and that something defines, instantiates, and otherwise gives material form to the learning that follows.

Claim 2: Learning as Learning Something. The second claim follows from the first: that learning, whether in reference to faculty work or anybody else's work, implies learning something, that talk about learning is vague and insubstantial when we do not know what it is that is being learned, including how the learning is framed, for learners, in terms of the knowledge at issue. To decline to specify what is learned may be as obfuscating as to decline to specify who is learning. Learning implies a learner (or learners). It also implies something (I will call it a subject) to be learned. This feature of the word *learning* complicates its meanings in that images of learning are likely to vary depending on who learners are, what they learn, and who is thinking about their learning (see Shulman, 1986, 1987, 2000, for discussion of the continuities between "subject" and subject matter learning; see Bransford, Vye, Kinser, and Risko, 1990, for discussion of dangers in views that dichotomize content and learning).

One reason for this complexity is that the what of learning (substance learned), along with the who of learning (a learner's unique interests and frames of mind at a given point in her or his life), help constitute its how (process and experience). Learning, in this view, is unique, dependent on what the learner knows at a moment in time about the unique subject being learned. This learning does not generalize as fully as is often assumed. We are relatively familiar with assertions about the uniqueness of learners, including how learners change over time or as they move from space to space (Gergen, 1991). We acknowledge, far less often, the uniqueness of what they learn, given that the diverse meanings, images, interpretations, foci, and contextualizations that any one person may bring to the scaffolding of her own knowledge will in all likelihood yield differences in meaning for the knowledge at issue. Thus, differences in understanding among persons struggling with meaning often occur: among authors and readers, teachers and their colleagues, teachers and students, students and their peers, and so on. Yet the problem is far more complex, since learning differences abound not only among individuals but also within them (for example, a person who may favor one subject over others), and also within subjects that differ substantively and structurally among themselves such that any person, regardless of personal interest in one subject or another, will have to switch learning gears in moving from learning one to another.

To appreciate the depth of these differences inherent in a learner's proclivities to learn one subject or another and inherent in the subject matters at issue, let us consider why ignoring them can be problematic. First, ignoring such differences may induce us to generalize, inappropriately, learners' experiences of their learning across multiple subject domains. Yet we know that individuals experience learning differently in different academic subjects, and the diversity of their experiences, as well as reasons for it, is deserving of attention. Individuals vary too in their experiences of the learning of professional practices, as when a practitioner-in-training develops some skills and insights on practice more easily and thoroughly than others. For example, an academic scientist may do very well in learning new lab techniques (defined as a practice or set of practices), yet learning how to mentor students about these techniques (defined as a different though related practice) may be hard for him. This difference merits attention for academic leaders and senior professors invested in this scientist's professional development.

Second, ignoring the differences in how any one person experiences the learning of diverse subjects and practices leads us to overlook the unique combination of tools and resources needed to access and explore the diversity of what is to be learned. What it takes to learn in one subject matter (that is, to see and understand it) will vary from what it takes to learn in others by virtue of the differences in the substance and form of the subjects themselves, as constructed historically and contemporaneously. For example, a student—let us call her Norah—might say the words, "It is hard to learn," in the context of her efforts to learn mathematics. Norah might say too that "it is hard to learn" in the context of learning psychology. She may say these words again about the experience of learning how to be a leader, how to be a parent, how to be a friend, or how to cook like a gourmet chef. However, the difficulty associated with each experience of learning—and importantly, the very sensation of learning for each "subject" at issue—differs, both with regard to the individual learner's (Norah's) proclivities to learn one thing as opposed to another (Norah may like literature better than math, or she may have better personal associations to narrative than numbers) *and* the "thing" itself being learned (the differences in the epistemic structure of the mathematics and psychology, both of which, though very different, she may find "hard" to learn) (Schwab, 1978). For Norah, learning in mathematics is likely to differ from learning in, say, English literature, not only because she happens to like literature and is able to access it better than math, but also because literature and mathematics, as forms of knowledge, are substantively and structurally (Schwab would say "syntactically") different subjects for anyone to learn, regardless of their likes and dislikes.

Learning does not happen in and of itself. For learning to occur, other entities must be present: there must be one or more learners, and there must be something to be learned. Without the "something to be learned," it is quite unclear what learning entails or even whether it happens. And similarly without the learner, it is unclear where the learning is, who is doing it, what its strengths and challenges are. Thus, the phrase *to learn,* in and of itself, is an abstraction. To give meaning and form to learning—to understand where learning does its work and what that work is—we must know both who is learning and what it is that such persons (or entities) are learning. (I credit my own learning of this subject to the pioneering work on teacher learning by Lee Shulman [see Shulman, 1986, 1987], in continuity with that of Joseph Schwab [1978] and John Dewey [1964].)

Turning to the cases for evidence of learning, I will focus on the substance of what it is that selected actors appear to be learning, that is, the subject of learning. Here are some of the things being learned in Elizabeth Creamer's case (Chapter Four). The research team is conducting a study of immigrant youth and families residing in a metropolitan area since the mid-1980s. Although we do not have much detail as to what about this population is being pursued or why, we must assume that certain features of this population are, in fact, the subjects of study. The team is constructing knowledge interactively, among themselves at least, about the lives of immigrant youths and families in an urban area. This is their subject, at least in a broad sense. Their knowledge construction endeavors, defined as learning, can be tracked through the layers of new knowledge that they uncover or create as they proceed with their work. Without attention to the substance of this research team's learning—its materialization and change over time—we cannot tell if learning happens at all for them.

Creamer provides other examples of learning and indicates the subjects of this learning (what is being learned) for the group as a whole and for its individual members. Consider Steven, the leader of the group that Creamer studied. Years back, Steven became "disillusioned" with the problems typically studied in his field; he saw them as relatively unimportant. As a result, he committed himself to the discernment and articulation of larger, more important problems—problems that he saw as mattering to people's lives, for example, reading achievement. Although we might see Steven's pursuit of reading achievement and related topics as the what of his learning now, allowing us thereby to track his learning within the subject matter of reading achievement, we can also imagine that part of his career-long journey involves the conceptualization of what an important research problem is and what it is not. In other words, in doing his research, Steven is learning not only about the subject matter of reading, but also about research as itself a subject matter, and with attention to the research issue of what constitutes an important research question. If we pursued Steven's autobiography further, we could explore the question of what features of a research topic might make Steven view that topic as important, and what features of a topic might lead him to view it as unimportant. Thus, for Steven, we have instances of an individual learning at least two things: reading achievement and the criteria of importance in research and what an important research question looks like.

Finally, given Creamer's analysis of the collaboration at issue, with attention to differences in members' thinking (and their valuing of particular forms of thought), we will be tempted to say that they are learning to collaborate. Though indeed they are, their learning to collaborate is entirely

contingent on their having a subject matter (the knowledge they are constructing and reconstructing) to learn—a subject matter within which, and
through which, their differences, even conflicts, take form and then somehow become resolved. In other words, in order to collaborate, a team must
have something to collaborate about; in this case, that consists of their
learning about immigrant youth and families in urban settings. Knowing
something about the subject matter that serves as the stuff of a team's collaborative learning (and without which both collaboration and learning
might be meaningless) helps us imagine the unique (in fact, ungeneraliz-
able) forms that team members' differences and conflicts may take, as well
as the cognitive and discursive moves that it takes to resolve them, or at
least to live with them.

Is learning, defined as the construction of knowledge about something,
at play in Marilyn Amey and Dennis Brown's case as well in Chapter Three?
We might say that at one level, the team whose work Amey and Brown discuss is striving to construct knowledge of how a community develops its
capacities to own and use a certain kind of resource center. Amey and
Brown talk extensively about the differences in view about the center that
marked the team's processes initially and the convergence in points of view
that appeared to take hold later. To appreciate this struggle to understand
and its eventual resolution, it might be helpful to trace the different images
of community capacity to own such a service center as instances of knowing as these materialized over time in the workings of the group. That
would help us understand the track of learning (as knowledge construction)
in this work group.

Michele Minnis and Vera John-Steiner in Chapter Five use a bilevel
imagery of learning as requiring a subject, preferably one that is well formed.
We review first the faculty-with-faculty learning that produces the program's
form and process. According to Minnis and John-Steiner, the Water Resources Program at the University of New Mexico has learned how to create
three course-based contexts for students who are learning water resources
management. Whether intentionally and successfully or not, these faculty
members appear to have learned how to interact with one another in distinctive ways in each of the three courses, at times fruitfully (as in the third,
Project, class) and at other times possibly less so (as in the first two classes).
The case simultaneously explores another layer of learning: that which
occurs among students, and between students and faculty, in the program
overall but especially in the third course, Field Project. In that course, students gain firsthand exposure to and involvement in the central subject matter of the course: how to assess, improve, and evaluate water resource
practices for communities in need. At this point in the program, the students
assume a hands-on assignment by taking on a water resources improvement
project in Honduras. Given the descriptions that Minnis and John-Steiner
provide, we, as readers, can "see" the students learning, but only because we
(like they themselves, and like their professors) are completely clear about

what it is that they learn (the subject matter of water resources management). The third course, then, reflects a palpable subject for the students' and faculty's learning. Their learning is less visible to us in the two earlier courses, possibly because their subject matter has not yet been fully conceptualized by the faculty who teach them, much as the student evaluations suggest. However, as the authors suggest, it may be necessary to analyze the clarity and meaningfulness of "subject" cumulatively, across the three courses, rather than on a course-by-course basis, since the success of the third course may represent cumulative effect.

What have we learned thus far about learning as portrayed in the three cases relative to the first two claims that I have made? The three cases highlight faculty as engaged in three forms of collaborative interdisciplinary work: outreach (Chapter Three), research (Chapter Four), and teaching (Chapter Five). Each of these three teams faces challenges unique to the subject matters and local problems with which faculty and others working with them, all as learners, must grapple (how to think about immigrant families and youth, how to conceptualize a community resource center, how to teach about water resources coherently yet through an interdisciplinary voice). In Creamer's and in Amey and Brown's cases, team members do not simply apply what they know—whether as research methodology or outreach design—in some direct and systematic fashion to problems in "the real world out there." Rather, they wrestle with each question and problem they encounter until they achieve some understanding of how best to respond to it. Although we do not have access to all of the conversations that ensued, we might hypothesize that the wrestling reflects a struggle to learn in a context within which one's own disciplinary moorings are suspended. We might also hypothesize that the substantive reshaping over time of these two groups' purposes for existence (that is, their agendas) comprises part of the substance of their learning. In both cases, we are helped to see the learning in process because we have fairly good access to what is being learned because something does in fact exist to be learned in each case.

In contrast, Minnis and John-Steiner portray a case whereby the work activity of the faculty (the imperative to get classes taught) may supersede experiences of learning how to carry out interdisciplinary teaching activity, especially in the Contemporary Issues and Models classes of the Water Resources Program. In these two classes, the faculty's learning about the subject of how to construct and teach an interdisciplinary program seems to be in the background. It contrasts sharply with the construction of a different, though not unrelated, subject (the subject matter of water resources) in the third, field-based class. The learning that occurs in the third class, for students and faculty alike, is more palpable, possibly because it is clear to all these learners that there is something to learn. The clarity of subject may be unique to the third course, or it may be the product, additively, of the three-course experience.

Claim 3: Interdisciplinary Practice as the Subject of Learning.
Bearing in mind the claim that faculty work implies the possibility of faculty learning of some thing(s) in particular, we move on to the third claim: that although the what of what is being learned is typically construed as knowledge (for example, subject matter), the what may also be construed as social and cultural practices. Harking back to our earlier example, we might view mathematics, psychology, leadership, parent-child relations, the essentials of a particular cuisine, and so on as constituting both knowledge and knowledge practices, that is, as ways of working with the knowledge at issue that are unique to that knowledge. For example, one who knows mathematics can work with mathematical knowledge in mathematical ways, which may be very different from working with history (in historical ways) or sociology (in sociological ways). She may thereby engage in mathematical practices (in contrast to historical, sociological, or other disciplinary practices). Given the unique meanings that mathematical knowledge affords and constrains, the mathematics at issue interacts as well with the learner— for example, responding in mathematical terms to the learner's mathematical actions. In other words, the subject matter of mathematics, as a product of a mathematical community, interacts with the learner's mathematical knowledge. Given the unique substance and syntax of mathematics, the learner of mathematics and the mathematical knowledge at issue interact within the terms of what is mathematically possible. (For further discussion, see Lave and Wenger, 1991; Wenger, 1998; Wenger, McDermott, and Snyder, 2002).

Thus, we might say that what faculty learn is not static, lifeless knowledge. Rather, professors learn a way of interacting with knowledge that in a sense "talks back" in a voice of its own, distinct by virtue of its unique patternings of affordance for and constraint on thought (Greeno, 1998). As knowledge workers, we might view professors as pushing on knowledge in diverse ways and through diverse media, even as, by virtue of its form, the knowledge (yes, as socially constructed) pushes back (Neumann, 1999). In this view, what a professor is learning is a knowledge practice—one perhaps already created by others, or being modified, or created anew—within a community of practitioners who have some shared view of what, together, they are "up to" in the name of practice. That community often has been in place for some time, as have the general outlines of its practices (see Wenger, 1998).

What might this idea of practice (as enacted by knowledge practitioners working within communities of bounded knowledge practices) look like in the context of professors' work? I respond with an example. When a professor of history is learning something new about history—that is, extending her knowledge of history, whether in the context of her research or teaching—she is, in effect, extending her competence as a practitioner of historical knowledge. In this view, the making, refining, or elaboration of historical knowledge (that is, historical ideas) is itself a practice (or a conglomerate of multiple practices) that is shared within a disciplinary community of practitioners of history—of people who work with historical knowledge and have skill in the shaping of historical meaning. In extending her understanding of history in particular historical ways, the historian is engaging in a social practice that she shares with others within a bounded community, the community of historians, or, more to the point, the community of practitioners of historical thought. Furthermore, she is accountable to them, and to the knowledge that they share, for her work, in that she must be able to make it known and somehow meaningful to them (Wenger, 1998). In this view, the what of what this professor is learning is not a static thing, with no vision or voice of its own, but a live practice, a knowledge construction that is made and remade and reflects back on its maker through the minds of others who participate in its making. The subject has a voice (Palmer, 1998) transmitted through the minds and voices of those who, through community, participate in its creation.

Yet we must acknowledge too that if a subject (or subject matter, knowledge construction) has a voice, then that voice is not likely to be consistent across a broad-ranging discipline or field—for example, across all who belong to the disciplinary community of history. Rather, a subject, and thereby a practice, is likely to vary to some extent across a community, across its constituent parts, possibly even from person to person, and certainly from time to time (see Becher, 1989; Clark, 1987). Thus, within the larger community of historians, smaller communities of specialized forms of historical practice may exist, differentiating themselves, by virtue of the unique meanings and aims of their practices, from other historical communities around them. In this more complex view of communities (and the meanings they represent) embedded within communities, the mega-community may begin to resemble "a constellation" (Wenger, 1998; Pallas, 2001), while its constituent communities, sometimes yielding newer communities from within themselves, may emerge as the loci of historical knowledge construction (Becher, 1989). To view the substance of what is learned as a practice within one or more of these embedded communities is to acknowledge the continuities of thought, and of minds at work with that thought, over place and time (that is socially, culturally, and historically)—continuities that define a practice as "of community." But also (and this is important) to view the substance of what is learned as a practice is to acknowledge its discontinuities—socially, culturally, and historically. Communities and persons, though linked to each other, individuate their practices even as they share in them. What this view helps us to understand is that the construction of knowledge cannot be construed as a solo act; it occurs among webs of people or within a web connected to other webs, as Amey and Brown refer to in their model in Chapter Three. Learning, or the construction of whatever substantive thought is at issue, occurs along the strands of this web of multiple webs, that is, along the lines of connection or collaboration that link individuals in cognitive and, as Creamer tells us, discursive ways (Chapter Four).

What echoes of substance learned, as constitutive of practice, do we see in the cases of interdisciplinary collaboration presented in earlier chapters? To what extent might the imagery I have just presented help to explain those experiences? It is fair to say that the cases presented in Chapters Three through Five involve people struggling to think beyond the patterns of thought that their own disciplinary communities afford. Thus, in the most immediate sense, the cases clash with the view of learning in communities of practice that I have just presented. The people in each of the three cases resist the knowledge practices that their prior established communities represent. Creamer's actors strive, for example, for an understanding of immigrant youth and family in urban settings that exceeds traditional disciplinary views of this subject. Amey and Brown's actors strive to break up established community knowledge by creating a resource center for improving community life. Minnis and John-Steiner's faculty participants strive to build a program and teaching structure that limits disciplinary dominance over the central problem of water resources management. Yet if we look again at the cases, we see that as these individuals resist their prior knowledge practices and their prior communities, they create modified practices, perhaps new practices, in fact, in a new community. They create social practices of interdisciplinary work in new communities of interdisciplinary practice.

The creation of new practices, and new communities, disciplinary or otherwise, is an appealing idea, and one that we hear quite often in talk about leadership and reform. But as these cases show, such creation is very hard. The creation of new practices when older ones are deeply rooted in our lives, and the creation of new communities wherein new practices can be created, take thought, time, energy, persistence, and, no doubt, great patience. Consider, for example, how hard the individuals in Creamer's study had to work and how long it took for them to derive and develop faith in the practices they invented: of validating diverging viewpoints by alternating authorship, thereby allowing publication of competing viewpoints on a subject of study. Consider also how this door-opening practice might encourage these researchers to teach each other in the future and to learn from each other—to advance each other's thinking—about their own views of a subject, perhaps leading them to the creation of still deeper knowledge practices. Although this team's future remains untold, we may surmise that their publishing practices created some spaces for persons of divergent views to explore and formulate still other practices from each other. They did so by exposing themselves to each other's thinking, by engaging with each other's thought, giving and taking and thereby learning. They did this even though each continued to hold tight to her or his own previously learned paradigm: Paula, the anthropologist, remaining committed to anthropological and constructivist views, and Chris, more entrenched in a positivist view, to his. Simply by reading each other's writing—and by talking about their substantive thoughts, exposing them to each other's scrutiny, participating in the questioning of them—Paula and Chris might encounter new thoughts or rethink their own.

Amey and Brown also offer insight into the complex work of establishing community practices that may allow still deeper creation of learning practices. At the end of what Amey and Brown call Stage One in their model, a break occurred in the cross-disciplinary clashes at play in the group under observation. Members of the work group, say the authors, began to talk in the third person, and their prior self-referencing was replaced with attention to what the larger community would want. Amey and Brown say that these dialogic moves helped create an intellectual neutral space, allowing the group to suspend the disciplinary clashes previously at play. In this "third space," so to speak—one that exceeded "my view" and "your view," focusing instead on the views and needs of a larger community—group members devoted more time to listening than "reloading." Members began to attend more to inquiry than advocacy; they gave more attention to thoughts beyond their own. We can hypothesize that amid the work of creating a community resource center, this team constructed a discursive practice unique to their experience: they established a team habit of talking in the third person and focused on community. And they created some common meanings among themselves (consider the local meanings of *guardianship*, a term not in use by the disciplinary communities to which team members belonged though arising as central within this particular research team context). In the midst of their activity, group members somehow created unique ways of talking and thinking together: new dialogic practices that perhaps constituted a beginning phase of their learning together. They started to talk and think in altered ways that might eventually allow them to go on with their substantive interdisciplinary work, digging more deeply into the ideas and issues at hand.

Learning, as an experience of creating knowledge-based practices, is also evident in the case prepared by Minnis and John-Steiner. I draw attention, in particular, to the learning captured within educational artifacts that students produce for the class—artifacts that imply systematic and crafted ways of carrying out specific professional acts with specific professional goals in mind. Through the Field Project class, students follow an established protocol of activity in the field site, part of which includes documentation in journals of their labors, interactions, talks, and thoughts. This practice is shared by all participants and serves as a locus for learning, a place where students can reflect on and analyze the sights and sounds to which their work has exposed them. Entries in participants' journals are then funneled, selectively and with particular goals in mind, into final project reports that record the educational practice in which students have been engaged. In Wenger's terms (1998), both the journal and the final report "reify" elements of the "participation" that the practice at issue has surfaced in participants' minds, thereby further defining, and publicly, the nature of that practice (water resources management and improvement). Just as the form of the practice is stamped on paper, so does it become stamped in people's minds as a view, and indeed, as an understanding, of what water resources management entails.

Claim 4: Context as, in Part, the Content of Learning. I have thus far established that the concepts of learning, substance of learning, and substance of learning as potentially a social practice provide insight into how professors come to know and otherwise create their work and careers. These concepts force our attention to the development of professors' thinking in and about their work: their teaching, research, service, and outreach; their thinking about the substance of these efforts, namely, the subjects for which they claim expertise. I turn now to the fourth claim, which addresses the contribution of context to the view thus far developed. To understand learning, with attention to the what of what is being learned (whether as knowledge or as social practice), requires a deep and comprehensive appreciation of context, or more pointedly, of contexts (Bronfenbrenner, 1979). (The converse applies as well: to appreciate the power of contexts to shape learning, we must understand both what is being learned and who the learners are; Gergen, 1991.)

What is context? Based on growing understanding of sociocultural theories, situated cognition, and the social-psychological ecologies of development, many reviewed in Chapter Two, I proffer the following summary view. We might view context most basically as sets of interlinked social, cultural, intellectual, and personal affordances (and patterns or absence thereof) within which a focal learning and developing person, relationship, or other entity is nested. This can be further probed: What is it about context defined in this way that makes it matter in learning? Or how does context get into a person's mind? Figuratively, how does context get under a person's skin? Drawing on the ideas of John Dewey (1964, 1997), I simply say that it is experience. It is the power of some elements of context (compelling to a learner) to enter human experience, consciously or subconsciously, and thereby shape experience, or knowing, in substantive ways. As such, we may propose the following: What mediates our learning, or affords it, are the experienced contexts of our lives (see, for example, Kondo, 1990; McAdams, 1993).

But what range of contexts and contextual experiences does this include for faculty in particular? What might count as experienced contexts, each shaping learning, for professors? Drawing on the range of literature in higher education, Lattuca lays out in Chapter Two some essential settings: society, cultures and subcultures, history, institutions, disciplinary communities—indeed, the ranges of places and times that all too often we discuss quite apart from the substantive learning that occurs in them, and that they are likely to shape, for students, professors, administrators, staff, and others involved in higher education. The contexts, in all their diversity, have the power to enter learners' experiences in compelling ways (whether for good or ill). They may afford substantive resources, or stamp patterns of their absence, on mind, shaping thereby what a person knows of her subjects of research and teaching or, more clearly, her areas of substantive expertise. They are likely to shape as well the less-than-substantive domains of her understanding (administrative work and other campus responsibilities that, though necessary, are not related to one's substantive agenda, yet must be "learned").

The point bears deeper attention. If experienced social contexts matter for professors' learning, what is the range of social relationships (defined as experienced contexts) that might count, in experience, in the shaping of learning? Let's look at the cases at hand. Amey and Brown in Chapter Three and Minnis and John-Steiner in Chapter Five portray university faculty learning about aspects of their work (outreach in the former, teaching in the latter) in the experienced contexts of relationships with colleagues. In the case by Amey and Brown, we may surmise that if students, post-docs, administrators, and community leaders and members are participating in the project as well, faculty participants are learning in the experienced context of relationships with all these people. Creamer's case in Chapter Four indicates further that experienced mentoring relationships also may serve as contexts for academics' learning. Yet there are other experienced contexts to consider as well. Studies beyond those represented here portray professors and scholars learning in the experienced contexts of diverse relationships: with friends and partners, with one's own parents and children, with leaders and administrators, with universities and other organizations well beyond one's employing university (for in-depth discussions of collaborative relationships as influential micro-contexts of developing academic thought, see Creamer, 1999, 2003; Creamer and others, 2001). Other still broader contexts—history, large-scale cultures, large-scale economic patterns—might shape what comes to a person's attention for learning, as well as what remains absent, and the experience of such contexts, or the experience of their absence, is likely to shape the learning of college and university faculty. And conversely, so too might the particularities of individual faculty members' life histories (their autobiographical pasts, lodged as these are in larger historical events) contribute to what a person attends to for academic learning and how that learning proceeds. Individuals' relationships with their own selves—their memories and self-understandings, or patterns of their memories suppressed—might well shape the subjects, questions, and passions that guide their subjects of study and of teaching and learning. My message in all this is that context, though expansive, as Lattuca shows us, is also inordinately deep and complex: it is social, cultural, historical. It shapes cognition, but by virtue of the emphasis on experience, context (like content) is itself an object of human cognition, and it too is an object of learning, an object of substantive formation, and an object to be taught. Context can shape what is learned and how, but learning may be able to shape context as well, at least in some part. (For a discussion of the multiple contexts that may frame the learning of academics, see Neumann and Peterson, 1997, and Neumann 2003, 2004.)

What evidence of the complexity of the contexts of professors' learning shows up in the cases? The case in Chapter Four identifies these learning contexts, among others: the context of life (Steven's history with his field of study, his decision to depart from research traditions in his field, Paula's history as Steve's mentee), the context of relational dynamics among colleagues and between mentors and those being mentored (Steven's ways of working with his group, the unique tensions that persist between Paula and Chris), past disciplinary learning (continuities of disciplinary thought in Steven's approach to research despite his self-distancing from his field, similar continuities for both Paula and Chris), and institutional context (a university that obviously encourages interdisciplinary research in local settings). Chapter Three reflects the following contexts as potentially shaping the learning at play: institutional context (a university that encourages interdisciplinary outreach and research conducted on it), historical context (unstated, but we can assume that the timing of this outreach effort makes sense in terms of both the university's and the larger community's history), the city or local community as context (local needs as articulated or discerned), relational dynamics of group members as context (patterns of clash and collaboration), and leadership context (articulated definitions of how to work together), among others. Chapter Five suggests as well the following contexts: a university, colleague community, and geographical area that values water resources management and improvement efforts; the established curriculum for the Water Resources Program; the students collectively, and in teams, as communities within which diverse forms of learning occur—be that learning about water resources or learning how to work with an interdisciplinary faculty team; the field site and its challenges; the creation of field notes in journals and the writing of final reports, among others. As these images suggest, content and context, though seemingly different, have ways of becoming intertwined, and context itself is likely to become deeply infused into the content of what is learned and known. It is thereby worthy of attention.

Claim 5: The Object of Collaboration (a Subject of Learning) as a Problem. To facilitate collaboration by faculty representing diverse disciplines, perspectives, interests, and points of view, it may be helpful to position the object of collaboration as a well-defined, authentic problem, itself "supradisciplinary" (that is, exceeding any one discipline's purview) though receptive to team members' concerted interdisciplinary (between disciplines) attention and action. The cases help illuminate this claim. Chapter Five shows that by the time faculty and students collaboratively get to the third course in the three-part course sequence (the field project, which requires authentic immersion and engagement in a local problem), prior course-based concerns (coordination, ability of faculty to work together in teaching) dissipate. In the field, group members, as diverse as they are, coalesce around authentic and, no doubt, serious problems of water resources management. When teaching about water resources in the first two classes, the instructors and students alike have no clearly defined, authentic problem to capture and direct their interests and interactions.

They have little to respond to in these early classes other than their own and each other's ideas, the discussion of which is relatively low stakes given that there is no problem to address. In the context of a high-stakes problem for a real population in need, the tenor of interdisciplinary collaboration changes as faculty and students work together to avail a Honduran population of an adequate water supply. (For related discussion, see Brown, Collins, and Duguid, 1989; Cognition and Technology Group at Vanderbilt, 1990.)

Chapter Three also supports the claim. As long as outreach team members attend to interpretations emerging from their own disciplinary views, even as they try to teach them to others on the team, little transpires to indicate interdisciplinary and collaborative progress. Yet at the point that the team chooses to suspend the purposeful articulation of discipline-centered views, they begin to make progress. In this case, members accomplish this refocusing by learning to speak in the third person and attending less to views of self than to the needs of another "body" that enters the room. That "body" is the larger community to be served by the center the team will create; it is as much a part of this team's "subject" as is the resource center being created (for a related metaphor, see Palmer, 1998). By attending to the community as though it had a voice of its own, the team diffuses the disciplinary arguments that members may hurl at each other; rather, they listen to the "object" of their collaboration, namely, what they refer to as "the community."

The case in Chapter Four echoes a portion of this process as well. Although team members do not need to refine or clarify the object of their study (perhaps due to the unique nature of research as a form of faculty work), they do need to diffuse colleagues' views when these threaten to dominate the process of the group or when they threaten to silence differing perspectives (consider the standoff between Chris and Paula). Toward this end, the team's shared authorship guidelines and practices open possibilities for team members of diverse disciplines to speak their minds through research: to draw on the processes of their minds, trained in diverse disciplines, to identify data-based patterns. These guidelines create a collaborative team reality based on a logic of turn-taking such that each research participant has an opportunity to lead in data analysis reflective of her or his point of view.

Collectively, these three team experiences suggest that professors' interdisciplinary collaboration may be supported in one or more of at least three ways: clearly defining a problem or project; formulating that problem or project so that it reflects needs, on the part of team members, to respond authentically to others' (equally) authentic needs; and establishing discursive practices (or rules of discourse) that literally turn down the volume of disparate disciplinary voices while keeping them all in the room, blending their resources usefully in the light of the problem at hand.

What Attention to Learning Helps Us Learn About Higher Education

Although *learning* is an oft-used word, we have not exploited its power to help us understand faculty work and careers or explored its positioning within higher education more broadly. I close by discussing what the use of a learning perspective may contribute to our understandings of both. First and foremost, higher education is a learning enterprise. We presume to develop students' learning through teaching, and society's learning through research and sometimes outreach, or education cast as public service. Given the centrality of these missions for higher education, it would serve us well to understand in depth a key activity that underlies them both, learning, given the diverse forms that learning may take.

To anchor our studies of higher education in our students' and society's learning suggests attentiveness to what people learn and want or need to learn, what colleges and universities can honestly offer for their learning, and what it makes sense to do, pedagogically and otherwise, to foster and otherwise enhance their learning of desirable subjects. Attentiveness to learning is likely to quickly crystallize what matters among the vast number of activities that comprise college and university life and draw on its resources, thereby signaling activities, roles, and events that need to be preserved and enlarged. I would speculate that attention to learning in one facet of the higher education enterprise (for example, attention to the faculty's learning) may, if encouraged, touch deeply other facets of the enterprise (for example, the learning of students). In this view, a professor who makes it her business to learn, whenever and wherever she can, is likely to carry that learning into classrooms (Neumann, 2000), where it may serve as a context for the learning of students, thereby supporting the teacher's efforts to teach. I suggest that rather than competing with her teaching, a teacher's learning, if pedagogically framed, has the power to intensify the learning of both teacher and students, to focus it not only on the substance at hand but also on consideration of how and why we know that substance as we do. A similar argument might be proffered for service and outreach as forms of faculty work. Rather than competing with this work, a professor's learning, if pedagogically framed, might intensify the learning of service and outreach participants, for example, as they come to focus not only on the substance of their work together but also on what that work means and how and why it matters.

My closing argument thus far has emphasized the possible benefits of attentiveness to learning to higher education practices. Yet it is hard to end on purely a positive note, for the switch to a learning perspective, in considerations of the diverse array of practices that comprise higher education, is hard. We may want to begin to instill this orientation among college and university practitioners by infusing it first into research on higher education.

But this is not easy, requiring change in what we attend to and how. For example, to infuse a learning orientation into the study of higher education would require close and consistent attentiveness to an elaborated version of my second learning claim in this chapter: that to learn is always to learn something, and that the something of learning has to matter to the learner. If we take this claim seriously, then we must question consistently what people are learning at any time, whether this is what they ought to be learning and care about learning, how their learning is proceeding, and what they make of it. This would apply equally to students in classrooms and professors in research labs, for it is their learning of subject matter that is ultimately at stake in higher education.

I will close with an example from my own research. When I consider the learning of professors in the early post-tenure career, I note that these scholars, most at the prime of their lives, want to be learning their subjects of study (for example, as instantiated in their research and teaching). Yet I note too that in this period of early midcareer, many are busily learning other things: how to teach large and diverse classes, how to mentor doctoral students and junior faculty, how to make a curriculum or a budget work, how to run academic programs and departments, how to balance their family lives and their own lives with the life of the university, among others. They are also learning how to orchestrate their learning in contexts that make specific learning demands on them in ways they did not feel prior to tenure that now have caught them quite by surprise. What I and my colleagues have learned in this study is that often professors' subject matter learning is interrupted, and sometimes forced aside, after tenure (Neumann, 2003). A major challenge of the early post-tenure career is to construct new spaces for one's continuing substantive learning or to reconstruct that substance in different (though personally meaningful) form. These larger acts of knowledge construction or reconstruction are themselves acts of learning, inspiring to some yet discouraging to others (see Neumann, Kadar, and Terosky, 2004; also Neumann and Terosky, 2003).

Without attention to learning—including awareness that to learn is part of a professor's work, that it always requires learning something, that it is a professional practice, that it is deeply touched by context, and that it demands authenticity—we may become confused about whether a person is learning at all. Even as professors slow or stop their learning in one facet of their work (for example, in their research), they may well be learning in another, though "subjects" we might not expect. For example, that a scientist stops learning the science to which she is deeply committed and that may, in fact, have earned her tenure, may mean that she is busily learning how to run the department she chairs, learning research methods to help her direct the dissertations of students who otherwise would be adviserless, learning how to manage an increasing load of large, nonmajor, undergraduate classes. That a beginning professor of English literature is not learning new content in support of his scholarly agenda may mean that he is learning instead how to manage the grading of one hundred essays a week, or how to advise undergraduates through a complicated curriculum, or struggling to make sense of his new service responsibilities. In addition to attending to the real work that faculty do and to the fairness of its distribution among diverse classes of faculty, it may behoove us to attend to the less visible learning in which professors must engage to learn that work (Neumann, 2003). In the long run, the quality of a faculty member's learning about faculty work is likely to define the quality of that work. It also may come to define the professional identity of the professor, for example, as professors who learn to do research come to do more and more research, while those who learn service come to engage increasingly in service activities. My final point is this: that a professor's learning, realized or not, may be the most telling feature of what that professor can become, including the kinds of contributions that she or he will make to the university, students, and society. It deserves our attention.

References

Baltes, P. B., and Staudinger, U. M. (eds.). *Interactive Minds: Life-Span Perspectives on the Social Foundation of Cognition.* Cambridge: Cambridge University Press, 1996.

Becher, T. *Academic Tribes and Territories: Intellectual Enquiry and the Cultures of Disciplines.* Bristol, Pa.: Society for Research into Higher Education and Open University Press, 1989.

Bransford, J. D., Vye, N., Kinzer, C., and Risko, V. "Teaching Thinking and Content Knowledge: Toward an Integrated Approach." In B. F. Jones and L. Idol (eds.), *Dimensions of Thinking and Cognitive Instruction.* Mahwah, N.J.: Erlbaum, 1990.

Bronfenbrenner, U. *The Ecology of Human Development.* Cambridge, Mass.: Harvard University Press, 1979.

Brown, J. S., Collins, A., and Duguid, P. "Situated Cognition and the Culture of Learning." *Educational Researcher,* 1989, *18*(1), 32–41.

Clark, B. R. *The Academic Life: Small Worlds, Different Worlds.* Princeton, N.J.: Carnegie Foundation for the Advancement of Teaching, Princeton University Press, 1987.

Cognition and Technology Group at Vanderbilt. "Anchored Instruction and Its Relationship to Situated Cognition." *Educational Researcher,* 1990, *19*(6), 2–10.

Cohen, D. K., McLaughlin, M. W., and Talbert, J. E. *Teaching for Understanding: Challenges for Policy and Practice.* San Francisco: Jossey-Bass, 1993.

Creamer, E. G. "Knowledge Production, Publication Productivity, and Intimate Academic Partnerships." *Journal of Higher Education,* 1999, *70*(3), 261–277.

Creamer, E. G. "Exploring the Link Between Inquiry Paradigm and the Process of Collaboration." *Review of Higher Education,* 2003, *26*(4), 447–465.

Creamer, E. G., and Associates. *Working Equal: Academic Couples as Collaborators.* New York: Routledge Falmer, 2001.

Dewey, J. *On Education.* Chicago: University of Chicago Press, 1964.

Dewey, J. *How We Think.* Mineola, N.Y.: Dover, 1997. (Originally published in 1910.)

Gergen, K. *The Saturated Self: Dilemmas of Identity in Contemporary Life.* New York: Basic Books/HarperCollins, 1991.

Greeno, J. G. "The Situativity of Knowing, Learning, and Research." *American Psychologist,* 1998, *53*(1), 5–26.

Greeno, J. G., Collins, A. M., and Resnick, L. B. "Cognition and Learning." In D. C. Berliner and R. C. Calfee (eds.), *Handbook of Educational Psychology*. New York: Macmillan, 1996.

John-Steiner, V. P. *Creative Collaboration*. New York: Oxford University Press, 2000.

Kondo, D. K. *Crafting Selves: Power, Gender, and Discourses of Identity in a Japanese Workplace*. Chicago: University of Chicago Press, 1990.

Kohn, M. L. "Unresolved Issues in the Relationship Between Work and Personality." In K. Erickson and S. P. Vallas (eds.), *The Nature of Work: Sociological Perspectives*. New Haven, Conn.: Yale University Press, 1990.

Krieger, S. *Social Science and the Self: Personal Essays on an Art Form*. New Brunswick, N.J.: Rutgers University Press, 1991.

Lampert, M. *Teaching Problems and the Problems of Teaching*. New Haven, Conn.: Yale University Press, 2001.

Lattuca, L. R. *Creating Interdisciplinarity: Interdisciplinary Research and Teaching Among College and University Faculty*. Nashville, Tenn.: Vanderbilt University Press, 2001.

Lattuca, L. R. "Learning Interdisciplinarity: Sociocultural Perspectives on Academic Work." *Journal of Higher Education*, 2002, 73(6), 711–740.

Lave, J., and Wenger, E. *Situated Learning: Legitimate Peripheral Participation*. Cambridge: Cambridge University Press, 1991.

Lin, X., and Schwartz, D. L. "Reflections at the Crossroads of Cultures." *Mind, Culture, and Activity*, 2003, 10(1), 9–25.

McAdams, D. P. *The Stories We Live By: Personal Myths and the Making of the Self*. New York: Guilford, 1993.

Menges, R. J., and Austin, A. E. "Teaching in Higher Education." In V. Richardson (ed.), *Handbook of Research on Teaching*. (4th ed.) Washington, D.C.: American Education Research Association, 2001.

Neumann, A. "On Experience, Memory, and Knowing: A Post-Holocaust (Auto)biography." *Curriculum Inquiry*, 1998, 28(4), 425–442.

Neumann, A. "Professing Passion: Views of Passionate Thought in Scholarship." Paper presented at the annual meeting of the American Educational Research Association, Montreal, Apr. 1999.

Neumann, A. "Toward a Profession of Learning: Exploring How University Professors Learn Their Subjects Through Teaching." Paper presented at the annual meeting of the American Educational Research Association, New Orleans, Apr. 2000.

Neumann, A. *Professors' Learning and Scholarly Identity Development in the Early Post-Tenure Career*. Unpublished final report submitted to the Spencer Foundation, Chicago, IL, December, 2003.

Neumann, A. "Toward Images of University Professors' Scholarly Learning: Contexts That Shape Intellectual Endeavor in Early Midcareer." Paper presented at the annual meeting of the American Sociological Association, San Francisco, Aug. 2004.

Neumann, A., Kadar, R. S., and Terosky, A. L. "I Get By with a Little Help from My Friends . . . Exploring Recently Tenured University Professors' Experiences of Colleagueship." Paper presented at the annual meeting of the American Educational Research Association, San Diego, Calif., Apr. 2004.

Neumann, A., and Peterson, P. L. (eds.). *Learning from Our Lives: Women, Research, and Autobiography in Education*. New York: Teachers College Press, 1997.

Neumann, A., and Terosky, A. L. "Toward Images of Reciprocity in Faculty Service: Insights from a Study of the Early Post-Tenure Career." Paper presented at the annual meeting of the American Educational Research Association, Chicago, Apr. 2003.

Pallas, A. M. "Preparing Education Doctoral Students for Epistemological Diversity." *Educational Researcher*, 2001, 30(5), 6–11.

Palmer, P. *The Courage to Teach: Exploring the Inner Landscape of a Teacher's Life*. San Francisco: Jossey-Bass, 1998.

Prawat, R. S., and Peterson, P. L. "Social Constructivist Views of Learning." In J. Murphy and K. S. Louis (eds.), *Handbook of Research on Educational Administration*. (2nd ed.) San Francisco: Jossey-Bass, 1999.

Putnam, R. T., and Borko, H. "What Do New Views of Knowledge and Thinking Have to Say About Research on Teacher Learning?" *Educational Researcher,* 2000, 29(1), 4–15.

Schön, D. A. *The Reflective Practitioner: How Professionals Think in Action.* New York: Basic Books, 1983.

Schön, D. A. *Educating the Reflective Practitioner: Educating the Reflective Practitioner for Teaching and Learning in the Professions.* San Francisco: Jossey-Bass, 1987.

Schwab, J. "Education and the Structure of Disciplines." In I. Westbury and N. J. Wilkof (eds.), *Science, Curriculum, and Liberal Education.* Chicago: University of Chicago Press, 1978.

Shulman, Lee S. "Those Who Understand: Knowledge Growth in Teaching." *Educational Researcher,* 1986, 15(2), 4–14.

Shulman, L. "Knowledge and Teaching: Foundation of the New Reform." *Harvard Educational Review,* 1987, 57(1), 1–22.

Shulman, L. "Students and Teachers: What Should They Know?" Address at a conference, "The Future of Education." Northwestern University, Evanston, IL, May 26, 2000.

Wenger, E. *Communities of Practice: Learning, Meaning, and Identity.* Cambridge: Cambridge University Press, 1998.

Wenger, E., McDermott, R., and Snyder, W. S. *Cultivating Communities of Practice.* Boston: Harvard Business School Press, 2002.

Wertsch, J. V., Del Rio, P., and Alvarez, A. (eds.). *Sociocultural Studies of Mind.* Cambridge: Cambridge University Press, 1995.

ANNA NEUMANN is professor of higher education in the Program in Higher and Postsecondary Education at Teachers College, Columbia University, in New York City.

7

Examples are provided about ways to change professional and ethical practices to promote the creation of a culture that facilitates and equitably recognizes collaboratively produced scholarship.

Promoting the Effective Evaluation of Collaboratively Produced Scholarship: A Call to Action

Elizabeth G. Creamer

It is November, and faculty members in my department somewhere are shocked to learn that a colleague's bid for tenure during his mandatory year has been denied by the department's promotion and tenure committee. The scuttlebutt in the hallways is that he did not have enough single-authored publications. Most of his publications were coauthored with a senior colleague who was doing his best to mentor him. He might be surprised to discover that most of his reviewers gave him little credit for his role in the work, even though he was identified as lead author in most of the publications. Three months later, we are slammed with another round of disquieting news. The college tenure and promotion committee turned down another case that had sailed through the department committee. Questions about collaborative relationships were at the heart of this item of unsettling news, just as they were in the first case. In the second case, the complaint that led to a split vote in the bid for promotion to full professor was, again, that the record showed too little single-authored work and too much coauthored work with students. The unfortunate consequence of all the collaboration was said to be that a convincing case had not been made that a distinct research agenda had been clearly established.

Academic reward and recognition systems are part of the discursive practices that shape faculty behavior. The reward system is defined as departmental and institutional policies and practices regarding the evaluation of faculty. The recognition system involves the wider national and international audience for faculty work. It is reputation and impact of work that is the primary criterion for faculty success (Fox, 1985).

The two vignettes bring to life the contradictory messages faculty members receive about how much collaboration is valued in the academic reward and recognition system. Some of the mixed messages faculty receive about collaboration include:

Contradiction 1: Early-career faculty members are often advised to collaborate with senior faculty to gain experience about the publication process and grant writing. But regardless of statements about the allocation of credit, the senior member of the team is likely to receive a disproportionate share of the recognition (Loeb, 2001).

Contradiction 2: There is a professional and ethical mandate for faculty members to mentor graduate students and introduce them to the publication and grant writing process. But unless the publications focus on the faculty member's line of inquiry, collaboration can dilute the sense that a clear line of research has been established.

Contradiction 3: An agenda for social justice may motivate faculty to try to find ways to give collaborators an equal voice. But citation practices and authorship conventions allocate primary credit to the lead author.

That one case that opens this chapter is of an early-career faculty member and the second of a faculty member far enough along in a career where collaboration is generally not considered to be as risky adds to difficulty faculty members face as they try to juggle the demands of the system of faculty rewards.

Given that it is not uncommon for questions about collaboration to be at the center of disputed bids for tenure or promotion, it is surprising how rarely collaboration is addressed in publications about faculty evaluation. Not only were the words *collaboration* and *coauthorship* surprisingly absent from the indexes of texts about faculty evaluation (for example, Braskamp and Ory, 1994; Centra, 1993; Glassick, Huber, and Maeroff, 1997), there were no major sections or chapters devoted to evaluating collaboratively produced scholarship. The assumption that scholarship and teaching are singular activities was implicit in the texts, just as it generally is in discussion about the research process. The absence of explicit references to collaboration in texts about faculty evaluation is a clear acknowledgment of the individualistic values that underlie the traditional academic reward structure. These values reflect the unstated assumptions that artistic and scientific creativity is the product of singular inspiration and genius (Abir-Am and Outram, 1987; Stillinger, 1991).

Collaboration and rates of coauthorship are growing in almost every academic field (Austin, 2001). Despite this trend, only a small percentage of institutions are giving serious attention to redesigning the criteria they use to evaluate research (Glassick, Huber, and Maeroff, 1997). This is evident in the finding that while 69 percent of the respondents reported reexamining the methods they use to evaluate teaching, only 34 percent reported the reexamination of the criteria used to evaluate research. Only 16 percent of the respondents from research universities reported that they had undergone examination of the methods used to evaluate research.

Professional and ethical practices need to be reexamined in order to ensure the creation of structures and practices that facilitate collaboration and equitable recognition (Kochan and Mullen, 2001). Kochan and Mullen frame the issue as one of social justice: "Dialogue is an essential element in creating a new culture in higher education that accepts, values, and rewards collaboration on at least an equal par with individual research. We believe that such dialogue is often compromised because the prevailing academic culture perpetuates inequities in authorship, even when people of good faith are working together" (p. 3). These authors are suggesting that a cultural change is required to reward collaborative work on par with individual scholarship.

This chapter addresses the absence of discussion about collaboration in the literature about faculty evaluation. It recommends steps individuals engaged in collaboration, academic administrators, journal editors, and leaders of professional associations can take to promote the effective evaluation of collaboratively produced scholarship. Table 7.1, near the end of this chapter, summarizes the ways collaborators, evaluators and external reviewers, and the professional association and journal editors can promote learning-centered collaboration.

An Agenda for Collaborators

Academics who employ a functionalist perspective and approach collaboration as a way to achieve efficiencies by dividing up the labor face a different set of challenges than do researchers who adapt a collaborative approach as a way to advance learning and achieve creative and theoretical insight. Academics with the functional perspective are often concerned with an equitable division of labor and the appropriate allocation of credit. Agreement about authorship guidelines, particularly what it means to be lead or first author, is a priority for members of this group. Evaluators of dossiers during the promotion and tenure process often voice concerns about the flip side of this perspective: that academics are padding their records with publications for which their contribution to the intellectual content was minor.

Academics who undertake collaboration primarily to promote learning have to reconsider not only how they approach the process but how they document it. The implications of the learning framework for this group of collaborators is pursued in the following section using examples from the case studies presented in this volume and from a number of published narratives that provide detailed descriptions of collective ways to approach interpretation (see, for example, Eisenhart and Borko, 1991; Wasser and Bresler, 1996).

Documenting the Collaborative Process at Multiple Levels. Among the challenges facing collaborators is the requirement for documentation at many levels, from memoing and field notes during the design, data collection, and analysis steps of the process, to a description of the strategies used to achieve collective interpretation in research publications, and extending to biographical statements prepared during the process of annual reviews and the preparation of dossiers for tenure and promotion. The added burden placed on collaborators for documentation has the potential to be offset by more equitable recognition.

Interactive Memoing. Embedded in the process of establishing a convincing case for the trustworthiness of qualitative research is the expectation that researchers be reflective about the analytical process and capture the evolution of thinking as it unfolds through memoing and field notes. Memos require reflexivity about the evolution of the design and analysis, as well as about relationships to participants and the setting (Bogdan and Biklen, 1992). A commitment to document both the product and process of collaboration can provide the structure to help teams focus their interaction on activities that contribute to learning rather than strictly to procedural matters that, while necessary, divert energy from the development of new ideas or new ways of thinking.

Erickson and Stull (1998) encourage an approach to teamwork in conducting ethnographic research that embeds interactive reflection throughout the life of a research project. They underscore not only the importance of the documentation provided by field notes, but also interaction and dialogue about the notes among team members from the onset of the project. Interaction among those involved on a research team can influence research outcomes as much as, if not more than, the research design (Schratz, 1993). Erickson and Stull's observations demonstrate one way that the process and product of collaborative research are linked. They highlight how early steps of the collaborative interpretive process are key to the move from an individual to team perspective: "Explicit attention to this [sharing of field notes] in the early going can set the stage for the transition from individual ethnographers who 'own' their own notes to team members who share corporate ownership of the insights and analysis produced by field encounters" (p. 25).

Interaction about field notes early in the process of data collection is one strategy to dilute a sense of ownership for the data that can become an obstacle to developing the collective vision that Marilyn Amey and Dennis Brown describe in Chapter Three.

External Evaluators. A number of other strategies can be used to document the process and products of collaborative efforts. Chapter Three describes the results of the authors' analysis when they were contracted to serve as external evaluators for a university and community agency partnership. They used interviews, observation, and document analysis to examine how the team members moved from an individualistic, disciplinary stance to an integrated interdisciplinary stance.

A Team Ethnographer or Historian. "Writing stories" that reflect how a particular text was constructed (Richardson, 1995) offer some additional ideas about how to document the collaborative process in ways that promote learning. The team of K-12 arts educators that Wasser and Bresler (1996) describe had a person who assumed the role of team "memoist," or ethnographer. Part of her responsibility was not only to record conversations but to invite members to pick up the thread of unresolved issues across meetings. This strategy was credited with creating the conditions for the team to move from an individualistic disciplinary perspective to a collective consciousness where collaborators were not only cognizant of different viewpoints but were willing to invest the energy to use them to develop a more complex or nuanced understanding. (I discussed the steps in this process more fully in Creamer, 2003.)

Bogdan and Biklen (1992) and Schratz (1993) also advocate strategies that promote collective self-reflection. In the page and a half that they devote to team research in their introductory text to qualitative research, Bogdan and Biklen advise that it is "worth hiring someone to research the researchers" (p. 212). A team historian or participant observer can help a team to bracket biases, address conflict, and critically reflect on thinking. Collective self-reflection can follow the action, be conducted at critical junctures in the process, or be embedded throughout the entire process (Schratz, 1993).

Documentation During the Process of Tenure and Promotion. The conceptual framework that shapes this book suggests that collaborators adopt a process for reflection that not only documents what was done but what was learned as well. Unanticipated outcomes may be one of the best measures that a team achieved synergy (Creamer, 2004). The authors of *Scholarship Assessed* add their voices to the call for reflexivity and for documenting both the process and outcomes of learning (Glassick, Huber, and Maeroff, 1997). Good documentation, they argue, "is dynamic, producing not merely a snapshot but a moving picture of why as well as what, the process as well as the products of scholarly work" (p. 49). In other words, good documentation can capture learning and change.

Glassick, Huber, and Maeroff (1997) note that as part of the process of evaluating faculty work, it is important to look for evidence that a scholar critically evaluates his or her own work and uses the evaluation to improve its quality. For collaborators, this suggests the inclusion of critical reflection about the impact of collaborative research and teaching on productivity in materials prepared for tenure and promotion dossiers. This would include reflections about the contribution of collaboration to learning, paradigm shifts, and the mastery of new skills.

Documentation in Publications. Acknowledging the contribution of collaborators has generally been treated simply as a matter of appropriate reward that follows ethical allocation credit. As important as this is to the individual careers of faculty, proper acknowledgment is also a matter of being honest with the reader. When details about the collective process of analysis and interpretation are provided, a reader has more information to judge the trustworthiness of a publication.

There are a number of ways collaborators can provide details about the collective process and the contributions of those listed as authors of a publication: unconventional approaches to listing the names of coauthors in a publication, footnotes or other forms of notation to acknowledge the contributions of collaborators, and an explanation for how collective interpretation was accomplished.

Unconventional Approaches to Naming Coauthors. Some academics and journal editors are resigned to the idea that there is no way to get around the limitations of authorship listing, where the first or lead author is assumed to have the most responsibility for the intellectual content of a publication. Arguments against changing conventions for listing authors are consistent with the position that trying to discriminate the contributions of collaborators is inimical to the spirit of collaboration (Hafernik, Messerschmitt, and Vandrick, 1997). A clear division of labor may simplify the process of awarding individual credit or recognition, but it promotes a sense of ownership and interferes with the development of a collective consciousness.

Others have argued that authorship conventions routinely shortchange collaborators (Tescione, 1998). Mirroring a concern voiced by quite a number of feminists and critical theorists (for example, Gottlieb, 1995; Kennedy, 1995), Kochan and Mullen (2001) argue for the importance of subverting traditional practices for listing authors: "We share our belief that collaborative authorship practice should address issues of fairness and justice, and include strategies to make authorship that is truly equal more accurately visible" (p. 1).

In order to make visible the equality of their contributions to the publication, this pair of collaborators proposes six creative ways to present authors' names. Some of them include textual forms, like listing names in a circle, that are not readily translatable in a citation. They settled on using an equal sign to link their names: Kochan=Mullen=Mullen=Kochan. They suggest that coequal authors with a third author in a more tertiary position could be designated using this format: Kochan=Mullen=Mullen=Kochan, author3. One advantage of this suggestion is that it would not be difficult for citation databases to reproduce this format. Textual devices that offer specificity about the roles played by coauthors is one step toward more equitable recognition and reward of collaboratively produced scholarship.

Citing Conventions for Multiple Authors. The citing conventions for multiple authors, particularly the use of *et al.* or *and others,* is another professional practice that marginalizes the contribution of collaborators. American Psychological Association (2001) conventions reproduce the assumption of a single author and a hierarchical relationship with the requirement that publications with three, four, or five authors be truncated to only the first author after the first reference in a text.

Unconventional approaches to formatting the names of coauthors in a publication would advance the legitimacy of collaborative work only if it also translated to changes in the citing conventions for multiple authors. This could easily be overcome by allowing coauthors to specify the appropriate citation pattern. For example, a notation to cite a publication after the first citation as author1 and author2, et al. would facilitate more equitable recognition when two coauthors want to communicate that their contributions to a publication are comparable.

In making these suggestions, my intent is to offer ways to address the concern of collaborators who struggle to find ways to communicate an equal contribution. It is not my intent to encourage the gratuitous addition of the names of authors who did not make a significant contribution to the intellectual content of a publication. I wish to encourage practices that allow readers to make a reasonable assessment of who is the author of different ideas presented in a publication and to make a judgment about the credibility of the process used to achieve these insights.

Footnotes or Other Forms of Notation to Acknowledge the Contributions of Collaborators. It is not uncommon, particularly in books, to find a footnote or other notation about the roles played by different contributors to a volume in the acknowledgments. For example, Bensimon and Neumann offer this brief explanation about their contributions at the end of the acknowledgments to their jointly authored book, *Redesigning Collegiate Leadership: Teams and Teamwork in Higher Education* (1993): "Bensimon and Neumann directed the study reported in this book jointly. Each made an equal, though different, contribution to the book, and the sequence of their names on the title page reflects only alphabetical ordering" (p. viii). Kochan and Mullen (2001) maintain that the disadvantage of a brief reference like this is that they are often ignored by readers, as they might be discounted by evaluators who encounter this kind of description on the materials included in a tenure or promotion dossier.

Margolis and Fisher, authors of *Unlocking the Clubhouse: Women in Computing* (2002) provide one of the best examples I have seen of an explanation of the roles and contributions of two authors to a jointly authored text. In the introductory chapter, they note:

As we began our research, we referred to our collaboration as insider-outsider model; at its conclusion there was no longer any insider or outsider. By interweaving our two perspectives—Jane's expertise in gender, feminism, and education and Allen's expertise in computer science and education—we have attained *a more layered understanding* of the gender gap in computer science than we had without each other's perspective. Each of us had key pieces of the puzzle the other lacked. Our collaboration has allowed us *to make vital connections*—between insider knowledge of computing and its culture and an insider's ability to see the unseen, between an emphasis on rigor and an ear for nuance, between quantitative knowledge and qualitative knowledge, and

between an academic understanding of gender inequalities and the daily experience of these inequalities. Looking at the problem from different perspective has *allowed us to see things that we would otherwise have missed.* [p. 11,
italics added]

My interest is in promoting the practice of providing more detailed
information about the contribution of authors to a collaborative text than
has been the traditional practice. In their remarkably compact passage,
Margolis and Fisher manage to account for the different skills and expertise each brought to the project, the process they used by interweaving
their perspectives, and the outcomes of their work (which I italicized in
the quotation).

Margolis and Fisher's introduction is an example of collective reflection that I believe belongs in the introduction of any coauthored book. A
description of the process used to achieve collective interpretation and
analysis can mitigate against misappropriation of credit. That this is difficult to capture without reflexive memoing is something the volume editors
and some of the chapter authors discovered when we attempted to recall the
synergy that first brought us together in a symposium in 2001 (Creamer,
Lattuca, Amey, and Neumann, 2002).

Richardson (1988, 1994, 1995), a sociologist who has been a leading
advocate of experimental texts in the social sciences, is critical of ethnographers who separate personal reflection from the "objective" or "factual"
account. An advocate of "writing stories" that provide more detailed accounts of the process required to produce texts than is customary,
Richardson argues that personal reflections are marginalized when they are
placed in a separate section. She provides a different perspective to what I
have advocated because she maintains, "Personal experiences, anxieties, and
fears are marginalized, written about in introductions, appendices, memoirs,
and 'reflections' sections of qualitative journals" (1988, p. 203). She prefers
an approach where comments about the interpretive process are interwoven
throughout the text.

Acknowledging the Collective Process of Interpretation. An explanation of
the contribution of coauthors to the analysis presented in an empirical
account is generally relegated to a token sentence or two about the strategies
co-investigators used to achieve a satisfactory level of inter-rater reliability.
Similarly, it is highly unusual to find coauthors who acknowledge differences
in interpretation or explain how competing explanations were reconciled.
The case study of the research team presented in Chapter Four reveals the
ethical dilemma that can be created when the merging of all authorial voices
to a single, collective "we" suggests agreement about key conclusions when
such agreement does not necessarily exist. The strategy that this team
deployed, to leave the presentation of the different interpretations to articles
in journals addressed to different disciplinary audiences, provided the vehicle for them to avoid reconciling their competing interpretations. (I present

an argument for multivoiced texts as an alternative strategy in Creamer, forthcoming).

Eisenhart and Borko (1991), an educational anthropologist and a psychologist, respectively, offer an unusually detailed account about how two academics sought to reconcile competing disciplinary paradigms and achieve an integrated conceptual framework. To address their differences, they invested time to educate each other about the central assumptions of their respective discipline. After designing a distinct set of research questions and collecting data separately, they moved to a collective vision by integrating their different concerns in a conceptual framework. They then tested the framework by applying it to explain specific observations of apprentice teachers. Of this critical decision, they noted, "We reasoned that by asking ourselves to provide *an* explanation for *an* incident (and over time accumulating such explanations), we would force ourselves to deal squarely with the intersections and discrepancies between our approaches" (p. 150). This pair of collaborators created a discursive strategy that gave them a way to integrate their different disciplinary perspectives.

Conclusions: Themes That Cross Chapters

The sociocultural perspective is used most frequently in the context of understanding the learning that occurs in the classroom. It is employed less frequently to consider how scientific insight is produced. As Lattuca so ably traces in Chapter One, the sociocultural perspective helps us to see that scientific genius and artistic creativity do not emerge in a vacuum. They occur, and can be inhibited, within the shadow of the discursive practices of academic disciplines and through interaction with a network of similar-spirited colleagues within the intellectual and political climate of the time. By insisting that the context be expanded to recognize a wider circle of influence beyond the individual creator, the sociocultural perspective can be said to serve a social justice agenda. In this way, the sociocultural perspective may provide the language and conceptual orientation to inspire professional practices that promote learning-centered collaboration and equitable recognition that avoids erasing or marginalizing the efforts of contributors who are not well established in the profession.

Two themes that emerge in different ways in the case studies presented in this volume are the role of different perspectives in learning and the impact of disciplinary socialization.

Conflict and Tension as Inherent in Interdisciplinary Collaboration. One of the key themes to emerge from the previous chapters is that conflict and tension are an unavoidable dimension of efforts that set out to approach scholarly questions from the perspective of multiple disciplines. This is not the conflict that first comes to mind when the topic of collaboration is raised. That might lead to unpleasant recollections of the initially enthusiastic colleague who later fails to follow through, who seems congenitally incapable of meeting a deadline, or who is willing to call a project complete long before you feel it meets your standards of quality. This conflict is not about procedural matters but about intellectual issues: the competition among disciplinary perspectives that we see in the case studies in Chapters Three and Four. This kind of behavior, as Amey and Brown explain, is partly the product of disciplinary socialization and an individualistic reward system that encourages what they have called Stage One, expert-based behavior in their model of interdisciplinary collaboration.

The collaborators presented in the case studies in Chapters Three and Four addressed intellectual conflict in different ways. The team involved in the outreach effort that Amey and Brown described were motivated to find ways to integrate their different disciplinary perspective. With the aid of a facilitative leader, they moved in that direction by finding an intellectual neutral space where they were able to internalize the concept and language of others. Members of the team described by Creamer were motivated to see their research findings from the vantage point of different disciplinary perspectives, but they conceptualized this largely in terms of addressing different audiences. Their conceptual framework did not require them to integrate their different perspectives. Dialogue promoted familiarity with each other's viewpoints, which eventually served to amplify, rather than diminish, differences. The outcome of this team's efforts illustrates that collaborators can produce an end product that accommodates diverse viewpoints without reconciling them or undergoing any fundamental changes to their own conceptual orientation (Creamer, 2003). This is what Amey and Brown would label as Stage Two behavior in their model of interdisciplinary collaboration.

The power of disciplinary socialization to influence team dynamics is evident in the case studies presented in this volume. Amey and Brown in Chapter Three characterize the early stages of interdisciplinary collaborative work as reflecting an expert model, where members remain firmly entrenched in their areas of expertise and disciplinary perspectives compete for dominance. Minnis and John-Steiner describe the sense of vulnerability academics socialized to the expert model experience when they are pushed to venture outside the safe zone of their expertise.

Tenacity to a disciplinary or experiential worldview and/or deference to another's area of expertise impedes the ability of collaborators to achieve a synthetic conceptual framework.

Strategies to Address Conflict. Teams use a number of discursive strategies to address differences in viewpoint productively. Some keep a project moving forward through compromise, accepting consensus as the end product, deferring to a standard such as considering the needs of their audience or what is best for the group, or by just "muddling through" (Creamer, 2003). The leader of the research team described in Chapter Four attempted to create a culture that normalized conflict by stressing, first, the potential new insight created at looking at a research problem from the different angles of multiple disciplinary perspectives and, second, by maintaining the stance that conflict is routine, to be expected, and manageable. Despite the team-teaching environment, some the students participating in the field study described in Chapter Five expressed disappointment that they did not receive consistent feedback and directions. The instructors in this project may have been able to anticipate students' unease by launching the course with repeated warnings that conflict and different perspectives are endemic to interdisciplinary work.

Strategies That Promote Learning and the Integration of Diverse Perspectives. The development of a collective, synthetic, or integrative conceptual is a key step in a learning-centered collaborative framework but one that few collaborators achieve. Amey and Brown identify it as the last step of their model of interdisciplinary collaboration, but admit that it is largely conjecture on their part because the outreach team they studied had not yet fully achieved it at the time they wrote their chapter. Despite intense interaction, the members of the research team described in Chapter Four were never able to reconcile their competing interpretations of one of their principal findings.

Integration or the development of what Amey and Brown called a "collective vision" can be defined as developing a more nuanced or complex vision of the phenomenon. It is accomplished through acquiring familiarity with others' points of view and exploring the implications of differences in perspective. This is a clearly a point where learning occurs. Minnis and John-Steiner defined it "as a matter of creating a new center and dynamic among separate disciplines." They characterize it as the operational path to interdisciplinarity. Students in their interdisciplinary field project demonstrated integration when they were able to apply theory to practice through action.

A Bridge Role. Two of the case studies provide an idea of how teams achieve the integrated or synthetic framework that is associated with learning and new insight. The teams described in Chapters Three and Five built integration into their organization by creating a mechanism for bringing different viewpoints together. Minnis and John-Steiner call it a "bridge role" and assert that someone on the team must "consciously and seriously" undertake this role of facilitating cross-disciplinary communication. Amey and Brown explain that during the third stage of their project, a subgroup was explicitly assigned the task of bringing different viewpoints together. In addition, some teams use a team memoist or ethnographer to encourage the team to revisit areas where differences of opinions persist. As Amey and Brown maintain and Lattuca has argued elsewhere (2001), the new synthetic frameworks created by teams tend to complement, rather than replace, earlier paradigmatic lenses.

Revising Professional Practice to Promote Learning-Centered Collaboration

Although models have been presented in various settings about factors that influence the effectiveness or sustainability of collaborative efforts, few studies offer in-depth analyses of collaborative research practices (John-Steiner, Weber, and Minnis, 1998). It is the very absence of accounts in the literature that document how teams learn together (as compared to how they work together, a distinction noted by Clark and others, 1996) that may explain why so little attention has been given to considering the different practices required not only to promote but to evaluate collaborative efforts involving research and teaching. Wasser and Bresler (1996) point to a promising area for future research when they argue that one reason models for evaluating collaboratively produced work are missing is that so little is known about the process of collective interpretation. Writing stories (Richardson, 1995) and other types of reflexive accounts are an important way that collaborators can be more transparent about the process of collective interpretation and writing.

Amey and Brown argue in Chapter Three for the importance of preparing graduate students to work effectively on teams and to develop the type of skills required to accomplish interdisciplinary synthesis. Similarly, Minnis and John-Steiner in Chapter Five suggest that graduate students may be in a better position to play a bridge role on teams than are most academics because they are not yet completely socialized to the "expert model" (see Chapter Four). Graduate students who have had exposure to cross-disciplinary course work may be in a particularly good position to make a significant contribution to the pursuit of different perspectives and the development of an integrative framework. More research is needed about the contribution of graduate students to learning-centered collaborative projects.

Throughout this chapter, I have suggested a number of ways that professional practice can be altered to create an academic culture that esteems collaborative work as distinct from but of comparable value to scholarship that is more compatible with the traditional, individualistic reward structure that has dominated academe. These are summarized in Table 7.1. My suggestions for professional disciplinary associations include a call to create awards that recognize collaborative scholarship that is conducted in a way that results in new insight and learning that emerges from the integration of different, but comparably powerful, areas of expertise. Other suggestions include reconsideration of the stylistic conventions for citing multiple authors.

Boyer (1990) blazed a new trail in the evaluation of faculty credentials when he advocated for expanding the definition of scholarship. Suggesting that the goal of diversifying faculty requires that standard definitions of scholarship be extended to include other arenas, including scholarship about teaching and outreach activities, Boyer identified four distinct but overlapping categories of scholarship that have not become part of the com-

**Table 7.1. Summary of Recommendations to Promote
Learning-Centered Collaboration**

Collaborators	Professional Associations and Journals
• Promote collective interpretation through interactive memoing and/or by having a team ethnographer or historian.	• Create awards to recognize collaborative activities that result in original outcomes.
• Explain the contribution of distinct areas of expertise to the analysis and outcomes in publications.	• Develop ethical standards to guide collaborative practice.
• Use creative ways to list coauthors and identify equal contributors.	• Lobby for changes in et al. citing conventions.
• Prepare written guidelines to document agreements about practices for acknowledging authorship.	• Add another dimension to Boyer's categories of scholarship (1990): the scholarship of research.

mon parlance about faculty scholarship: the scholarship of discovery, the scholarship of integration, the scholarship of application, and the scholarship of teaching. The addition of a fifth category, the scholarship of research, has the potential to encourage additional research about processes and skills that lead to creativity and new insight.

References

Abir-Am, P. G., and Outram, D. (eds.). *Uneasy Careers and Intimate Lives: Women in Science 1789–1979.* New Brunswick, N.J.: Rutgers University Press, 1987.

American Psychological Association. *Publication Manual.* (5th ed.) Washington, D.C.: American Psychological Association, 2001.

Austin, A. "Reviewing the Literature on Scholarly Collaboration: How We Can Understand Collaboration Among Academic Couples." In E. G. Creamer and Associates, *Working Equal: Academic Couples as Collaborators.* New York: Routledge-Falmer: 2001.

Bensimon, E. M., and Neumann, A. *Redesigning Collegiate Leadership: Teams and Teamwork in Higher Education.* Baltimore, Md.: Johns Hopkins University Press, 1993.

Bogdan, R. C., and Biklen, S. K. *Qualitative Research for Education: An Introduction to Theory and Methods.* Needham Heights, Mass.: Allyn and Bacon, 1992.

Boyer, E. L. *Scholarship Reconsidered: Priorities of the Professoriate.* Princeton, N.J.: Carnegie Foundation for the Advancement of Teaching, 1990.

Braskamp, L. A., and Ory, J. C. *Assessing Faculty Work: Enhancing Individual and Institutional Performance.* San Francisco: Jossey-Bass, 1994.

Centra, J. A. *Reflective Faculty Evaluation: Enhancing Teaching and Determining Faculty Effectiveness.* San Francisco: Jossey-Bass, 1993.

Clark, C., and others. "Collaboration as Dialogue: Teachers and Researchers Engaged in Conversation and Professional Development." *American Educational Research Journal,* 1996, 33(1), 193–231.

Creamer, E. G. "Interpretive Processes in Collaborative Research in Educational Settings." *American Exchange Quarterly,* 2003, 7(3), 179–183.

Creamer, E. G. "Assessing Outcomes of Long-Term Research Collaboration." *Canadian Journal of Higher Education,* 2004, 34(1), 24–41.

Creamer, E. G. "Experimenting with Voice and Reflexivity in Social Science Texts." In C. Conrad and R. C. Serlin (eds.), *SAGE Handbook for Research in Education: Engaging Ideas and Enriching Inquiry*. Thousand Oaks, Calif.: Sage, forthcoming.

Creamer, E. G., Lattuca, L., Amey, M., and Neumann, A. "Supporting New Forms of Faculty Work." Interdisciplinary symposium presented at the Association for the Study of Higher Education National Conference, Sacramento, Calif., Nov. 2002.

Eisenhart, M. A., and Borko, H. "In Search of an Interdisciplinary Collaborative Design for Studying Teacher Education." *Teaching and Teacher Education*, 1991, 7(2), 137–157.

Erickson, K., and Stull, D. *Doing Team Ethnography: Warnings and Advice*. Thousand Oaks, Calif.: Sage, 1998.

Fox, M. F. "Publication, Performance, and Reward in Science and Scholarship." In C. J. Smart (ed.), *Higher Education: Handbook of Theory and Research*. New York: Agathon Press, 1985.

Glassick, C. E., Huber, M. T., and Maeroff, G. I. *Scholarship Assessed: Evaluation of the Professoriate*. San Francisco: Jossey-Bass, 1997.

Gottlieb, A. "Beyond the Lonely Anthropologist: Collaboration in Research and Writing." *American Anthropologist*, 1995, 97(1), 21–26.

Hafernik, J. J., Messerschmitt, D. S., and Vandrick, S. "Collaborative Research: Why and How?" *Educational Researcher*, 1997, 26(9), 31–35.

John-Steiner, V., Weber, R. J., and Minnis, M. "The Challenge of Studying Collaboration." *American Educational Research Journal*, 1998, 35(4), 773–783.

Kennedy, E. L. "In Pursuit of Connection: Reflections on Collaborative Work." *American Anthropologist*, 1995, 97(1), 26–33.

Kochan, F. K., and Mullen, C.A.K. "Collaborative Authorship: Reflections on a Briar Patch of Twisted Brambles." *Teachers College Record*, Feb. 12, 2001. http://www.tcrecord.org, ID no. 10661.

Lattuca, L. R. *Creating Interdisciplinarity: Interdisciplinary Research and Teaching Among College and University Faculty*. Nashville, Tenn.: Vanderbilt University Press, 2001.

Loeb, J. "The Role of Recognition and Reward in Research Productivity: Implications for Partner Collaboration." In E. G. Creamer and Associates (eds.), *Working Equal: Academic Couples as Collaborators*. New York: RoutledgeFalmer, 2001.

Margolis, J., and Fisher, A. *Unlocking the Clubhouse: Women in Computing*. Cambridge, Mass.: MIT Press, 2002.

Richardson, L. "The Collective Story: Postmodernism and the Writing of Sociology." *Sociological Focus*, 1988, 21(9), 199–208.

Richardson, L. "Writing: A Method of Inquiry." In N. K. Denzin and Y. S. Lincoln (eds.), *Handbook of Qualitative Research*. Thousand Oaks, Calif.: Sage, 1994.

Richardson, L. "Writing-Stories: Co-Authoring 'The Sea Monster,' a Writing-Story." *Qualitative Inquiry*, 1995, 1(2), 189–203.

Schratz, M. (ed.). "From Cooperative Action to Collective Self-Reflection: A Sociodynamic Approach to Educational Research." In M. Schratz (ed.), *Qualitative Voices in Educational Research*. Bristol, Pa.: Falmer Press, 1993.

Stillinger, J. *Multiple Authorship and the Myth of Solitary Genius*. New York: Oxford University Press, 1991.

Tescione, S. M. "A Woman's Name: Implications for Publication, Citation, and Tenure." *Educational Researcher*, 1998, 27(8), 38–42.

Wasser, J. D., and Bresler, L. "Working in the Interpretive Zone: Conceptualizing Collaboration in Qualitative Research Teams." *Educational Researcher*, 1996, 25(5), 5–15.

ELIZABETH G. CREAMER *is associate professor of educational research in the Department of Educational Research and Policy Studies at Virginia Tech in Blacksburg, Virginia.*

INDEX

Back Issue/Subscription Order Form

Copy or detach and send to:

Jossey-Bass, A Wiley Imprint, 989 Market Street, San Francisco CA 94103-1741

Call or fax toll-free: Phone 888-378-2537 6:30AM – 3PM PST; Fax 888-481-2665

Back Issues: Please send me the following issues at $29 each
(Important: please include ISBN number with your order.)

_____

_____

_____

$ _____ Total for single issues

$ _____ SHIPPING CHARGES: SURFACE Domestic Canadian

		Domestic	Canadian
First Item		$5.00	$6.00
Each Add'l Item		$3.00	$1.50

For next-day and second-day delivery rates, call the number listed above.

Subscriptions Please __ start __ renew my subscription to *New Directions for Teaching and Learning* for the year 2___ at the following rate:

U.S.	__ Individual $80	__ Institutional $170
Canada	__ Individual $80	__ Institutional $210
All Others	__ Individual $104	__ Institutional $244

Online subscriptions available too!

**For more information about online subscriptions visit
www.interscience.wiley.com**

$ _____ Total single issues and subscriptions (Add appropriate sales tax for your state for single issue orders. No sales tax for U.S. subscriptions. Canadian residents, add GST for subscriptions and single issues.)

__Payment enclosed (U.S. check or money order only)

__VISA __ MC __ AmEx #_____ Exp. Date _____

Signature _____ Day Phone _____

__ Bill Me (U.S. institutional orders only. Purchase order required.)

Purchase order # _____

Federal Tax ID13559302   **GST 89102 8052**

Name _____

Address _____

_____

Phone _____ E-mail _____

For more information about Jossey-Bass, visit our Web site at www.josseybass.com

greater civic participation. This volume describe FLCs from a practitioner's perspective, with plenty of advice, wisdom, and lessons for starting your own FLC.
ISBN: 0-7879-7568-0

TL96   Online Student Ratings of Instruction
Trav D. Johnson, D. Lynn Sorenson
Many institutions are adopting Web-based student ratings of instruction, or are considering doing it, because online systems have the potential to save time and money among other benefits. But they also present a number of challenges. The authors of this volume have firsthand experience with electronic ratings of instruction. They identify the advantages, consider costs and benefits, explain their solutions, and provide recommendations on how to facilitate online ratings.
ISBN: 0-7879-7262-2

TL95   Problem-Based Learning in the Information Age
Dave S. Knowlton, David C. Sharp
Provides information about theories and practices associated with problem-based learning, a pedagogy that allows students to become more engaged in their own education by actively interpreting information. Today's professors are adopting problem-based learning across all disciplines to faciliate a broader, modern definition of what it means to learn. Authors provide practical experience about designing useful problems, creating conducive learning environments, facilitating students' activities, and assessing students' efforts at problem solving.
ISBN: 0-7879-7172-3

TL94   Technology: Taking the Distance out of Learning
Margit Misangyi Watts
This volume addresses the possibilities and challenges of computer technology in higher education. The contributors examine the pressures to use technology, the reasons not to, the benefits of it, the feeling of being a learner as well as a teacher, the role of distance education, and the place of computers in the modern world. Rather than discussing only specific successes or failures, this issue addresses computers as a new cultural symbol and begins meaningful conversations about technology in general and how it affects education in particular.
ISBN: 0-7879-6989-3

TL93   Valuing and Supporting Undergraduate Research
Joyce Kinkead
The authors gathered in this volume share a deep belief in the value of undergraduate research. Research helps students develop skills in problem solving, critical thinking, and communication, and undergraduate researchers' work can contribute to an institution's quest to further knowledge and help meet societal challenges. Chapters provide an overview of undergraduate research, explore programs at different types of institutions, and offer suggestions on how faculty members can find ways to work with undergraduate researchers.
ISBN: 0-7879-6907-9

NEW DIRECTIONS FOR TEACHING AND LEARNING IS NOW AVAILABLE ONLINE AT WILEY INTERSCIENCE

What is Wiley InterScience?

Wiley InterScience is the dynamic online content service from John Wiley & Sons delivering the full text of over 300 leading scientific, technical, medical, and professional journals, plus major reference works, the acclaimed Current Protocols laboratory manuals, and even the full text of select Wiley print books online.

What are some special features of Wiley InterScience?

Wiley Interscience Alerts is a service that delivers table of contents via e-mail for any journal available on Wiley InterScience as soon as a new issue is published online.

EarlyView is Wiley's exclusive service presenting individual articles online as soon as they are ready, even before the release of the compiled print issue. These articles are complete, peer-reviewed, and citable.

CrossRef is the innovative multi-publisher reference linking system enabling readers to move seamlessly from a reference in a journal article to the cited publication, typically located on a different server and published by a different publisher.

How can I access Wiley InterScience?

Visit http://www.interscience.wiley.com.

Guest Users can browse Wiley InterScience for unrestricted access to journal tables of contents and article abstracts, or use the powerful search engine.

Registered Users are provided with a *Personal Home Page* to store and manage customized alerts, searches, and links to favorite journals and articles. Additionally, Registered Users can view free online sample issues and preview selected material from major reference works.

Licensed Customers are entitled to access full-text journal articles in PDF, with select journals also offering full-text HTML.

How do I become an Authorized User?

Authorized Users are individuals authorized by a paying Customer to have access to the journals in Wiley InterScience. For example, a university that subscribes to Wiley journals is considered to be the Customer. Faculty, staff and students authorized by the university to have access to those journals in Wiley InterScience are Authorized Users. Users should contact their library for information on which Wiley journals they have access to in Wiley InterScience.

ASK YOUR INSTITUTION ABOUT WILEY INTERSCIENCE TODAY!